Black Manifesto for Education

Black Manifesto for Education

Edited by Jim Haskins

With an Introduction by Mario Fantini

William Morrow & Company, Inc.
NEW YORK   1973

Haskins, James, (date)
    Black manifesto for education.

    Includes bibliographical references.
    1. Negroes—Education—Addresses, essays, lectures.
I. Title.
LC2801.H33 1973   370   72-13020
ISBN 0-688-00029-0
ISBN 0-688-05029-8 (pbk)

To My Father

Foreword

by Mario D. Fantini

Dr. Fantini is Dean of Education of the State University College at New Paltz, N.Y. He has served as a Consultant to the Fund for the Advancement of Education of the Ford Foundation, where he directed a project to identify and record effective teaching practices with disadvantaged elementary school children. In May, 1965, he joined the regular staff of the Ford Foundation, where he is a Program Officer. He has served as a consultant on many city, state and federal education programs and task forces. Among his numerous publications are Making Urban Schools Work, *coauthored with Gerald Weinstein;* The Disadvantaged: Challenge to Education, *coauthored with Gerald Weinstein;* Designing Education for Tomorrow's Cities; *and* Toward Humanistic Education: A Curriculum of Affect, *edited with Gerald Weinstein.*

The decline in quality urban education came to national awareness long before the Report of the Riot Commission said in 1967: "Particularly for children of the racial ghetto, the schools have failed to provide the educational experience which could help overcome the effects of discrimination and deprivation."

In hard data the evidence of failure is irrefutable. In New York City, 30 percent of *all* children are reading more

ix

than two years behind grade level in grades six through nine, as measured by standardized tests. In predominantly Negro and Puerto Rican schools, the percentage is even higher. And New York is not alone. High unemployment, confinement of the semi-educated to entry level jobs, the low number of academic diplomas in the ghetto reinforce the point.

Because the problem has been so widely acknowledged in professional circles—to say nothing of growing public awareness—an enormous amount of effort has been spent in attempts to intervene and break the spiral of educational decline and failure. Many of these original attempts, however, were little more than a study or description of the problem with few "prescriptions" or recommendations for alternative courses of action. The focus was on the problems of the learner. "Cultural Deprivation" was examined, for example, but rarely was the connection made between this knowledge about the learner and the teacher's actions in the classroom.

Nonetheless, a few prescriptions eventually emerged, and the search began for teaching practices and materials relevant to inner city students. Occasional attempts have been made not only to know the learner, but to respond to him by diagnosing his needs, concerns, and cognitive (intellectual) and affective (emotional) learning styles. Despite these findings, rarely have school programs been adjusted accordingly.

Meanwhile, new urban dynamics are developing faster than relevant teaching and quality education. The population of big city school systems is no longer white middle class. Students, parents, and particularly the nonwhite community are becoming alienated and visibly disturbed by the performance of the schools. Impatience with cumbersome school systems insensitive to the needs of students has led often to bitter controversy, reaching a peak in 1968 during which 44 percent of all civil disorders in the six riot-prone cities in the United States involved educational institutions.

It has become increasingly apparent to many intimately or even remotely involved with education that fundamental reform of schools is needed and that the central concern of public schools in big cities must be the education of Blacks. It is also apparent that no single formula for reform will alleviate the problems—there can be no "either-or" solutions.

In the past decade, there has been a flurry of attention to the problems of the poor on the part of both the professionals and the public. We now have complete new categorizations, such as urban education, the disadvantaged, the culturally deprived, white racism, self-determination, desegregation, integration, community control, decentralization, compensatory education, and so forth. The biggest attention has been given to the education of Blacks. Despite all the attention given to this problem, very little has actually been accomplished with the majority of Black learners. It is one of the major disasters facing American education, and this is due, in part, to the fact that many of the definitions, classifications, and assessments made on the problems of Blacks have been made by Whites. While this may have been understandable, and while many Whites had good intentions, it is quite clear that enormous gaps in perception and sensitivity are apparent when Whites try to deal with Black experiences. Consequently, one of the important aspects of this book has to do with the fact that we are now beginning to have Black educators speak about Black issues. Especially those who are White, who have the privilege of reading this book, will see that the perceptions of a prominent group of Black contributors to this volume will set a tone that is quite different from those that have been set conventionally, that is, by concerned White educators (of which I am a member).

Contributors to this volume are impressive, not only because they have made important contributions to the field and have achieved high status, but because most of them are "action oriented" professionals. That is to say, the contributors to this volume are in the action as "involved observers," to use the term coined by Professor Kenneth Clark. Many of them still occupy these action roles: presidents of boards of education, superintendents of schools, teachers, and so forth. Not only is this a book by Black educators, but it is by a group of practitioners. As practitioners who have occupied important positions in the educational establishment which has victimized so many Black educators, their reporting is vivid and to the point.

Consequently, this group of Black educators is quick to pinpoint the basic problems. First, they point out that the diagnosis of the educational problem has been wrong. We have held that the problem is with the learner, his family, and background. For the past decade, we have called the educational casualty "deprived" or "disadvantaged." This type of diagnosis has led to faulty prescriptions, e.g., compensatory education. Trying to rehabilitate the learner to fit the standard school has produced little gain. In fact, President Nixon himself pointed to the failure of compensatory education:

> The best evidence available indicates that most of the compensatory education programs have not measurably helped poor children catch up.

> Recent findings on the two largest such programs are particularly disturbing. We now spend more than $1 billion a year for educational programs run under Title I of the Elementary and Secondary Education Act. Most of these have stressed the teaching of reading, but before-and-after tests suggest that only 19% of the children in such programs improve their reading significantly; 13% appear to fall behind more than expected; and more than two-thirds of the children remain unaffected—that is, they continue to fall behind. In our Headstart program, where so much hope is invested, we find that youngsters enrolled only for

the summer achieve almost no gains, and the gains of those in the program for a full year are soon matched by their non-Headstart classmates from similarly poor backgrounds.*

The compensatory diagnosis and prescription have been made by those in positions of responsibility, mainly White.

These compensatory forms of intervention to help so-called "Black children" learn are quickly exploded in this book. The myth is exploded, that is, that any type of classification of Black children as "culturally deprived" or "disadvantaged" (or anything else) that surfaces from the White sentiment results in Black children's not learning (self-fulfilling prophecy). This group of analysts makes absolutely clear that the problem is not with the "Black learner," but with the school itself, its basic structure and educational process. This is the new diagnosis. As might be expected, they are not completely agreed on the prescriptions that follow this diagnosis. Some favor integration with a mainstream that has made it. Others feel that the mainstream itself is corrupted, and that Blacks ought to consider greater control of institutions that serve the unique interests of Black people.

The question of institutional racism is obviously a matter of great concern, but, here again, there is no blanket indictment of Whites. In a classic study of the Washington, D.C., Public Schools, Professor Kenneth Clark gives the impression that the institutional structure itself has conditioned a type of racism which affects not only Whites, but Blacks, as well. This emphasis on institutional dysfunction, especially as it pertains to the survival needs of Black people in this country, is made passionately clear.

This book makes increasingly apparent to those concerned

_____

* Nixon, Richard M. *Message from the President of the United States to the 91st Congress*, 2d Session, Document No. 91–267, March 3, 1970.

with the improvement of education that a new strategy for educational improvement has to be devised for the seventies and beyond. We have learned some important lessons in the sixties which should be useful, providing us some guidance. One of the first lessons is the realization that the caption "disadvantaged" is of limited value to us as a diagnostic tool when the learner is viewed as the problem. That is to say, the learner is disadvantaged because there is something lacking in him, his background, his culture, and so forth. Rather, a more useful view for us to assume in the decades ahead would be to view "disadvantaged" as a function of *institutional* shortcomings.

To put it simply, the school as a social institution does not have the capacity to deal with human diversity, that is, educating everyone, in a pluralistic society. Therefore, anyone who participates in this type of institution is in a sense disadvantaged. This position helps explain why so many White suburban so-called advantaged learners have apparently "turned off" on the public schools.

The second lesson, related to the first, can be simply stated as that we have expected the learner, regardless of his background, to adjust to the school, rather than the other way around.

Thirdly, the school has devised an educational process which necessitates everyone's being treated with a sense of sameness. This adjustment to sameness has come into direct conflict with the basic reality of human and group differences. Consequently, conflicts between the uniqueness of the individual and cultural pluralism and community style, have come into direct conflict with the established norms of the school. These lessons, together with many others, lead us to the conclusion that the educational strategies which we employed in the sixties were, indeed, based on a faulty diagnosis.

Our attempts to remedy the problems for those classified as "disadvantaged" amounted to rehabilitation through programs of concentrated remediation. This approach, known as compensatory education, while helping many individual children, has *in toto* produced very little difference. However, it did provide us with a base of experience and a necessary stage for education to go through.

The crucial point for us at this time is that to continue for the seventies is to guarantee further frustration and failure. To deal with the complex problems of institutional reform in the seventies will necessitate a systematic orientation from those most concerned with the problem.

This collection also points out that the climb from powerlessness is greatly dependent on quality education. As a major institution, the public schools literally can determine who can "make it."

Public schools as community-based institutions can become important agencies for breaking the cycle of despair in which the majority of Blacks find themselves. This cycle, poverty, poor education, poor jobs, and so forth, insures a dependent status to those caught within it. Further, the public school structure permits only those Blacks to enter the White controlled mainstream who are ready to accept White or western values.

However, the struggle for self-determination and freedom which has been waged in this society for hundreds of years has reached a new stage of expression. Increasingly, Black communities—especially among the young of the current generation—are articulating the need for Black unity, for a consolidation around the distinctiveness of the Black experience, for a coherence generated by the style and culture of a Black nation—segregated by an alien White society.

No aspirations, whether acculturating with White or Black unification, can be accomplished without quality education taking place in public schools. Some argue that this quality can only come when Blacks control these schools—so that they can be made to work for the welfare of Black communities.

Others want quality education by holding accountable who-
ever happens to be inside the schools—Black or White.

This collection also reveals that there are divergent positions among Blacks concerning the most appropriate strategy
to embrace in the next encounter with public school reform.

We obviously need more books like this one, and Jim
Haskins is to be commended for his ability to assemble such
a wide spectrum of talents on one of the most pressing problems facing the nation. I certainly would encourage Whites
to read this book, especially Whites concerned with problems
of improving education, for in an ironic sense, the beginning of what is being proposed in this collection would
improve not only the education of Black and other minorities, but the education of all children.

Contents

Only the educated are free.

—EPICTETUS (*c.* A.D. 100)

Black Manifesto for Education

I

Blacks and Urban Education

1

Preparation for Life: The Black Classroom

by Isaiah E. Robinson, Jr.

Isaiah E. Robinson, Jr., was appointed a member of the Board of Education in 1969 by Manhattan Borough President Percy Sutton, becoming President of the Board in 1971. He is currently serving as Chairman of the Board of Education's Committee on Decentralization. In addition to serving on the panel of the Bundy Commission on Decentralization and in the White House Conference "To Fulfill These Rights," Mr. Robinson has served as consultant to the "Continuing Education" project of the Chicago Urban League at Chicago University, the Instructional Administrators Program at Fordham University, Teacher Training at Hunter College, College of New Rochelle, New York City College, and the Teacher Corps. He has also served as educational consultant to the Borough President of Manhattan and several State Assemblymen from Manhattan. He was President of the Harlem Commonwealth Council for Economic Development and an adviser to the IS 201 Governing Board.

In addition he has been a Director of the Public Education Association and an Associate Director of the Harlem Freedom School for the study of Afro-American History and Culture. He is the author of a report, "Operation Excellence," on community control of schools in the ghetto, and an article, "Educational Determinism" (Liberation *magazine, 1968).*

Part I

IN OUR TIMES

Since World War II the American school has had two goals: integration and participatory democracy. From the Fair Deal to the Great Society—a period of great activity, excitement, and anticipation—numerous legislative measures and appropriations have been directed toward accomplishing these laudable objectives. Unfortunately, however, Black Americans, despite rising expectations, have enjoyed only the dregs of such efforts. The true beneficiaries, according to all indices, have been white Americans, whether native born or one hour naturalized. The Federal Housing Administration and the Small Business Administration alone can claim the distinction of creating dependent colonies of powerless Blacks, surrounded and controlled by bedroom communities of parasitic suburbanites. Looking back, we find that segregation, discrimination, and oppression have escalated over the last twenty-five years.

The American school was instrumental in developing the rationale and mechanism through which this was accomplished. When the veterans returned from World War II and created a surplus labor force, the ingenious rationale of the Credential Society was devised. The diploma became the prerequisite for employment and could be used as a screening and sorting device to insure a "better class of employees"—a most effective way of maintaining the century-old policy of racism.

Thus Blacks are still excluded from economic progress through effective discrimination in education and employment.

What little Black prosperity that does exist today is as accidental as it was during World War I and II, when Blacks were employed in many occupations, not because they were wanted but because they were needed. Credentials are now required to do the same jobs, experience is less important, and Blacks are forced out of the job market, thereby swelling the ranks of the unemployed. The foundation laid centuries ago by an alien race that is not disposed to worry about the economic survival of anyone but itself remains. For example:

> An applicant to the apprenticeship program of a local steamfitters' union undergoes a battery of four tests to qualify. In one of them he is called on to answer questions such as the relationship between Shakespeare and "Othello," Dante and the "Inferno," and Walt Whitman and poetry.
>
> His facility with vocabulary is tested by words like "modiste" and "debutante" and by the challenge to match such terms as "verity" with its opposite—"myth." The aspiring steamfitter also finds himself asked to associate Dali with painting.
>
> Although such questions have nothing to do with steamfitting, the particular test in which they appear has managed to weed out two-thirds of all non-white applicants for the apprenticeship program while serving to disqualify less than one-fifth of the white candidates.

Over the years, social scientists have engaged in learned disputes about whether heredity or environment made the Black child an inferior human being. (Note however that their basic assumption of Black inferiority is never disputed.) For example: Arthur J. Jensen and his supporters do not doubt that genetic factors are largely responsible for the fact that Black children have lower average IQ scores and poorer scholastic performances than white children. The perennial debate vainly continues to emphasize superiority and inferiority, culture and lack of culture, privilege and underprivilege, and advantage and disadvantage. Regardless of where emphasis is placed, however, the national policy of exploiter and exploited is maintained. To discuss Black intelligence and achievement without referring to the manifold ways in which white society has systematically stripped Blacks of their past, ambitions, and sense of self (as Jensen does) is to ignore the most important factor of all—RACISM, a subject people refuse to talk about because they cannot cope with it. As a result, Americans live with and condone a preposterous lie.

Black children are increasingly articulate in expressing their skepticism about their schools and what is taught in them. They take for granted that "The Big Lie" is shoved down their throats not only by their teachers, but by politicians, the government, and even their parents. Where did this "paranoid" view come from?

Black children live in ghettos, but they are told about American affluence. Their fathers, brothers, and cousins are sent home in wooden boxes from a patently immoral war, but they are told about the fight for freedom. They know that suburbia is inaccessible to them, but they are told about fair housing and freedom of mobility. They witness police brutality, but they are told about law and order and American justice. In other words, they trust their own senses, feelings, and experiences and distrust what they are told. Why not? How do we justify such disparities to them?

Such disparities are particularly sharp between the impoverished Black communities and the suburban bedroom communities that surround them. When classroom experiences in the two communities are compared, the contrasts are downright offensive, but they do provide insights into the Black child's skepticism. Vast numbers of Black children live in environments that teach them they are inferior and that for generations their families have held an inferior position in society. They are referred to as "them," "those children," "wild animals," and other similar terms. Their own attitudes and those of others discourage them from developing motivation, drive, and effort. Their teachers do not believe they can learn, do not expect them to learn, and do not try to help them learn. Injuries are being inflicted by those who claim to motivate and teach them, who have in reality alienated them and destroyed their identity through subtle and not so subtle rejections of their culture, leaving ultimately those whom nobody values. How can equal education exist if Black children are considered innately defective?

It is the teacher's responsibility to develop a sense of self-worth and competence in all his students. Most teachers, however, regard Blacks as a segregated, servile caste with restricted rights and privileges. Even the courts deal with Blacks both in Law and Custom on a different and peculiar basis. Inevitably, these attitudes must result in lawlessness in the classroom. Many researchers claim that the differences between poor and good schools are not related to innate pupil intelligence or community efforts, but to the amount of money spent on them. The federal government has provided billions of dollars for compensatory education programs for the so-called disadvantaged. New York City, for example, has received more than $500 million since 1965 for one such program, Title I, Elementary and Secondary Education Act (national legislation initiated by President Johnson in response to pressures and protests by Blacks throughout the nation culminative in massive school boycotts—N.Y.C.). Yet the retardation in the average classroom for Black children in New York City has increased from approximately 60 to 85 percent. This shocking disclosure can only be understood in terms of how effectively the national policy of racism has been implemented.

Presumably, compensatory programs across the country have the pedagogic motive of preparing Black children to become part of the larger society, but the national policy dictates unpedagogic motives like control, order, and keeping Black children from competing in an economy that does not want or need them. In other words, the $500 million allocated to New York City has made the already affluent more affluent, and, until equal opportunities in education are assured, future proposals for such programs should be rejected.

The Black child does not want money; he wants love, sympathy, and above all, respect, untainted by sordid greed or cheap vanity. The teacher's role is not to keep him in his place but to lift him out of the crippling defilement of the places where segregation and discrimination, the national policy, has relegated him.

Only their own kindred and race can bring these gifts to the Black classroom. With few exceptions, they are the men and women with the spirit, deep devotion, and determination who can succeed in teaching Black children despite such bitter difficulties. They are less harsh and pessimistic in their evaluation of Black children because they come from similar backgrounds and have managed to attain positions of responsibility and status in spite of racial barriers. Black teachers historically come from the top ranks of academic achievement and are representative of the few Blacks who are allowed access to higher education by a society that offers them few economic choices, usually teaching and preaching, which become a lifetime career.

The reverse is true for white teachers. The field of education has the reputation of attracting students who want the easy path to a degree. Education majors as a group tend to be poorly motivated, which is revealed in their classroom efforts. Numerous research studies have shown that education majors consistently score lower scholastically than other college students. Forty years ago, Learned and Wood compared college seniors in education with randomly selected high school seniors and found that many of the high school seniors actually scored higher in the subjects the education majors were supposedly prepared to teach. In 1965 Harvey reported that today's education majors have not improved substantially. Such candidates, armed with their passport to work, man Black classrooms, and their own lack of motivation is compounded in those classrooms.

The high turnover and dropout rates for teachers also contribute to low-quality performance in Black classrooms. For every one-hundred college graduates who satisfy the New York State teacher requirements, ten to twelve of them are found in the classroom ten years later. The explanation is that the most talented teachers leave the school system for better paying positions and the so-called "trousseau teachers" find mates.

It is plain from the evidence that education for Black children is no longer merely inadequate, it is now almost hopeless. The alarming degree to which the school system has failed Black children moved W. Willard Wirtz, former United States Secretary of Labor, to state:

> We are piling up a human scrap heap . . . many of whom never appear in the unemployment statistics. The human scrap heap is composed of persons who, as a consequence of technological development . . . and educational failures . . . are disqualified from employment in a skilled economy.

Black parents view the present conditions in education and say in amazement, "What has happened? The school was successful with masses of illiterate Irish, Jews, and other white ethnic groups who stormed these shores. Why are the classrooms dysfunctional now when the majority of students, not only in New York City but in other large cities as well, are Black?" It is sufficient to say that all attempts to desegregate the schools in the North, South, East, and West have been frustrated because the dominant society has hardened its resolve to defend the political and economic advantages and privileges derived from its undemocratic social arrangement.

Black parents' efforts to end segregation and improve their schools have ended in numerous confrontations and mass frustration; their struggles have been well documented and need not be explored here. After decades of sustained struggle for civil rights, Blacks face the realization that their position is worse than at any time since the Emancipation Proclamation. This is the crisis in urban education!

> When you have succeeded in dehumanizing the Negro, when you have put him down to be but as a beast . . . when you have extinguished his soul in this world and placed him where the ray of hope is blown out as in darkness of the damned, are you quite sure that the demon you have roused will not turn and rend you?
>
> —Abraham Lincoln

Part II

AN OVERVIEW

Education has played a central role in the dreams and frustrations of the Black American since the Declaration of Independence was signed. Like his white counterpart, he has viewed the school as the gateway to opportunity. Yet while holding out the promise of a democratic society, with liberty and justice for all, the school has functioned as a barrier against it. This fact, however, has not dampened the tenacity with which Blacks pursue that promise.

From the beginning, Americans have depended on their schools to produce patriotic citizens, good government, and solutions to the country's social, economic, and political problems. After two hundred years, they still expect the schools to perform these functions. President John F. Kennedy's inaugural address expressed the importance of education to Americans in the following words:

> Our progress as a nation can be no swifter than our progress in education. Our requirements for world leadership, our hopes for economic growth, and the demands of citizenship itself require the maximum development of every young American's capacity. The mind is our fundamental resource.

If the President's statement is true, and if the United States is to become a just and humane country, then the American school must abandon its strategy of containment of Black youngsters and begin developing their minds.

The school is a social institution and as such imposes a variety of inevitable pressures on all who are exposed to it. A just society must have conventions, rules, and laws in order to provide its citizens with full and equal opportunity to realize their potential for usefulness and happiness and to reduce social friction between groups and individuals. In America, however, these rules, conventions, and laws are grounded in a national policy of subverting change and perpetuating two societies, one white and one Black, with whites prospering from the exploitation of Blacks.

The United States Constitution and the Bill of Rights provided a positive framework for citizenship and freedom, but the question of whether the Black man was to be included in this framework was unsettled for more than seventy-five years after the War of Independence. The Emancipation Proclamation of 1863 proclaimed the Black man's freedom, the Thirteenth Amendment to the Constitution secured that freedom, the Fourteenth Amendment made him an American citizen, and the Fifteenth Amendment provided penalties for any state that denied his rights of citizenship because of race, color, or previous condition of servitude. These rules should have been incorporated into the socializing processes of the American educational system so that both Black and white children could realize their potential and participate fully in a democratic society. In actuality, the schools perpetuated a society that was elitist, racist, conformist, repressive, authoritarian, status-conscious, middle- and upper-class oriented, and white male chauvinistic. Even a cursory examination of American history makes these facts obvious.

Any break in the color line would mean a loss of profits and a dismantling of selectively restrictive and status-oriented career opportunities for whites; in other words, segregation was highly profitable. Thus two school systems were needed: one that failed to teach the Black child and one that succeeded in teaching the white child. After two centuries of this social policy, both whites and Blacks are justified in feeling that the American school has achieved its goal.

All available evidence corroborates the existence of two school systems. Classrooms faithfully mirror the racial bias, economic discrimination, and overt and covert types of social discrimination found in the larger society. Discrimination is incorporated into the classroom by numerous methods such as "tracking," "ability grouping," or "incentive promotions," all of which serve to separate white and Black students. Thus the schools have made certain that future positions in finance, commerce, industry, and government will be filled by whites.

Consider the following facts: According to the 1966 census, only 42 percent of the students who entered high school graduated and, of this group, less than 8 percent graduated from college. The proportion of students forced out of school before the twelfth grade continues to be high and the majority of them are Black. Little imagination is needed to realize that this sorting and screening process happens not by accident but by design.

Segregation is the primary stratagem in this scheme. What better way is there to fill young hearts and minds with feelings of inferiority, self-hate, and worthlessness than through isolation, separation, or segregation. Segregation means poverty, teeming racial ghettos, men and women without jobs, families without men, and classrooms that drive children to the street, crime, narcotics, dependency, and welfare. Where are all the conventions, rules, and laws that would remedy these conditions? Have the Constitution and Bill of Rights been exorcised? Was the Supreme Court decision of 1954 just a dream?

It would be unfair to call all white Americans conscious racists—many of them have revolted and cried out in protest—but race tyranny, aristocratic pretense, and monopolistic wealth continue to be the product of our classrooms. Recognizing the existence of these realities is only the beginning. One must ask how they have persisted through centuries of legal, moral, and other forceful attempts to change them, and why the one institution that is called the gateway to opportunity and fulfillment is the very one that most effectively perpetuates the oppressed and impoverished status of Black Americans?

The entire school milieu is imbued with a muddy kind of racial and class morality, replete with all its prejudices and false virtues. Consequently, if social class and race are considered together, it is possible to gain greater insights into why teachers are unable to reach and teach Black children. They expect Black children to fail, and the children fulfill that expectation.

In too many classrooms, the tactic commonly used to discourage Black children from achieving is to expose them to constant insults and humiliation, which block their learning and reinforce the sense of worthlessness instilled in them by the society outside. Their subconscious awareness of this tactic evokes burning anger and hostility that divert their energies from learning into ways of striking back.

Teachers will argue vehemently that this assertion is not true and that the low achievement of Black children is caused by their deplorable living conditions and culturally deprived family backgrounds. Dr. Kenneth B. Clark refutes such reasoning and declares that "Black children do not learn because they are not taught." Teachers not only teach their Black students less, they also apply lower standards when evaluating their achievement and behavior. Individual attention is out of the question—the bright, average, and dull students are all systematically retarded in one way or another.

Let us rule out the notion of a conspiratorial social policy, and let us assume that teachers are well intentioned and diligently apply their considerable skills to educating Black children. Then how do we explain the fact that they unwittingly help perpetuate such a grossly inequitable system? Eleanor Burke Leacock has described in detail how different the expectations of teachers of Black and white students are with regard to academic achievement and behavior and how these expectations serve to teach Black students *not* to learn. The name of the game is self-fulfilling prophecy. The teacher transmits the following message to Black children in myriad ways: "This is your place in society; act, perform, talk, and learn according to it and no more." Thus he gets no more and no less than he expects from his students.

Black students sense what is happening and develop a variety of defenses to protect themselves. Because they are compelled to attend school, they must do so to survive. Some withdraw into apathy and persuade themselves that they do not care. More often than not, such children are labeled as emotionally disturbed or problem children. Others act out their frustrations by rebelling against the system and are expelled as a result. Generally, however, Black students adopt the strategy of conformity and docility, which is not only encouraged but often demanded by teachers and administrators. Under such conditions it does not take the Black student long to realize that getting through schools means suppressing his feelings and emotions and subordinating his own interests and desires to those of his teacher and other authority figures. In this way he is prepared to enter society.

A different approach is used with the white student. The preconditioned class and race-oriented, middle-class teacher and student understand each other; they speak the same language, share the same world, eat the same foods, psychic and otherwise. Because society expects the white student to succeed and rewards him for doing so, he generally acts according to those expectations.

Today's environment is more dangerous than that found in any other era. "We live in a society that is vicious, crafty, dishonest, immoral, irreligious, and corrupt—a society that is competing for its own destruction." Kent State, Jackson State, the Black Panther purge, and now Attica are prime examples which force us to conclude that this society condones such behavior. The American classroom must assume much of the responsibility for these realities.

2

Education and the Making of the Black Urban Ghetto

by John Henrik Clarke

John Henrik Clarke was born in Union Springs, Alabama, and grew up in Columbus, Georgia. He went to New York City in 1933 with ambition to pursue a career as a writer. After four years in the U.S. Air Force, where he was a sergeant major, he attended New York University and majored in history and world literature. Also, beginning with his early years, Mr. Clarke studied the world history of African people.

As a fiction writer he has published over fifty short stories in magazines in this country and abroad. His best known short story, "The Boy Who Painted Christ Black," has been translated into more than a dozen languages. His articles and conference papers on African and Afro-American history and culture have been published in leading journals throughout the world. He has served as a staff member of five different publications and was co-founder and associated editor of the Harlem Quarterly *(1949–1950).*

Among the other positions he has held are: feature writer for the Pittsburgh Courier *(1957–1958), Research Director of the first African Heritage Exposition (August, 1959), Associate Editor,* Freedomways *magazine (1962–Present), Director, Heritage Teaching Program, HARYOU-ACT (1964–1969), and Special Consultant and Coordinator of the C.B.S.*

16

*TV Series, "Black Heritage: The History of Afro-Americans"
(1968). Presently Mr. Clarke is an Associate Professor in the
Department of Black and Puerto Rican Studies at Hunter
College, New York City, and a Distinguished Visiting Pro-
fessor of African History at the Africana Studies and Research
Center at Cornell University. Mr. Clarke has written or
edited thirteen books. The best known are* American Negro
Short Stories *(1966),* William Styron's Nat Turner: Ten
Black Writers Respond *(1968), and* Malcolm X: The Man
and His Time *(1969).*

The subject is both topical and historical, and, to understand
it, we will have to look at it both ways. We will have to
acknowledge that the long sore of the slave trade, colonialism,
and formalized racism is still a lingering influence in black
ghetto life. The black ghettos are servants' quarters for the
white people who control power in this country. There is
no way to understand the role of education and the making
of the black urban ghetto without also understanding the
servants' quarters and the servants that I have alluded to.
When servants are educated at all they are educated to serve,
but never to share power. This is the basic dilemma in black
education. Black people were not brought to this country
to be given education, citizenship, or democracy—they were
brought to this country to serve, to labor, and to obey.

Now, let us look at the present through the lens of the
past—let us look at the long roots of this dilemma.

During the fifteenth and sixteenth centuries Europe awakened from the lethargy of the Dark Ages and began to project
itself into the broader world. For more than a thousand years
the Africans had been bringing into being empire after empire, until the second rise of Europe; then, internal strife
and the slave trade turned what was an "age of grandeur" to
the Africans into an age of tragedy and decline. Certain
events in Europe and in Africa set this period in history in

motion. In the chain of events that were to follow, no year is more important than 1492. Christopher Columbus opened up the "New World" for European settlement. The Europeans, mainly Spanish and Portuguese at this time, were searching for new materials and markets, new manpower, and new lands to exploit. The African slave trade was created to accommodate this expansion. Had there been no market for the slave there would have been no slave trade. The market and the motive helped to create the vast plantation system that followed. The Europeans needed a rationale and the Christian church gave it to them before the slave trade was well under way. In a little known though very important Papal Bull of 1455, the Pope authorized Spain and Portugal to "reduce to servitude all infidel people." The Pope told the Europeans now entering the slave trade that they did not have to feel guilty for what they did to non-Christian people. This Papal Bull and others that followed would later help to lay this basis for Western racism and the massive dehumanization of most of mankind. The writer Eric Williams analyzes this period in history in great detail in his book *Capitalism and Slavery*. Dr. Williams shows how the idea of race developed concurrently with the slave trade and the rise of modern capitalism.

In his book *Race, Science and Humanity,* Dr. Ashley Montagu refers to the belief in race as a "widespread contemporary myth in the Western world." He further states, "It is the form of the older belief in witchcraft."

In another book, *Race: The History of an Idea in America,* the writer Thomas F. Gossett shows how racial theories were gradually developed to accompany already existing racial prejudice. The book begins in this manner:

> When English colonists first landed in this country, they immediately encountered one race "problem" in the Indians. In a few years they imported another when, in 1619, the first boat load of Negro slaves arrived. What had been

the history of ideas about race up until this time? Is the problem of race an age-old one in human relations, or is it mainly as a result of revolutions of thought in biology and anthropology which took place in the eighteenth and nineteenth centuries?

In addition to answering his own question, Mr. Gossett traces the history of racism in this country from its beginning in the English colonies to the eve of the Second World War.

Racism has affected every aspect of Afro-American life, especially education and housing. When the first "free" blacks began to separate themselves from the chattel slaves, they lived mostly in separate communities that were small ethnic ghettos. These blacks began the search for the kind of education that was relevant to their survival. The slaves had education of a sort—education that prepared them to serve their masters more profitably. This education was mostly through apprenticeship. Out of it a large number of slave craftsmen emerged. Some Africans already had basic skills when they were brought to this country.

Among the black abolitionists and other "free" blacks in the north, education became the prime objective and the great obsession. They wanted it for themselves and freedom and education for the blacks still enslaved. Out of this struggle a responsible group of black radical freedom fighters emerged. These are the men that Lerone Bennett referred to as "Pioneers in Protest." They began the search for the lost African heritage; they led or inspired the massive slave revolts during the early part of the nineteenth century. Their agitation against the system of slavery continued until the eve of the Civil War. After this war and during the period called Reconstruction, some of these men became the leaders of black America. Education was the main theme of their public speeches and writings.

The Reconstruction era is one of the most written about and least understood episodes in American history. For the black Americans it was the period of a new beginning. New hope and new illusions were rampant. The blacks in leadership actually thought that America would, at least, keep its promise to all of its people.

In the opening chapters of his great book, *Black Reconstruction in America,* Dr. W. E. B. Du Bois had stated: "Easily the most dramatic episode in American history was the sudden move to free four million black slaves in an effort to stop a great war, to end forty years of bitter controversy, and to appease the moral sense of civilization."

Dr. Du Bois is talking about the end of one era and the beginning of another. His explanation continues: "From the day of its birth," he says, "the anomaly of slavery plagued a nation which asserted equality of all men, and sought to derive powers of government from the consent of the governed. Within the sound of those voices who said this lived more than half a million black slaves, forming nearly one-fifth of the population of a new nation."

Slavery was the contradiction between the American promise and its fulfillment. Dr. Du Bois, like a number of other black historians, saw the Reconstruction Era as the time when a fragmented nation made the first serious attempt to come together and put its house in order.

In the preface to his book, *Black Power U.S.A.,* the historian Lerone Bennett, Jr., gives the following brief overview to the Reconstruction:

> At the end of the Civil War, America embarked on a racial experiment unprecedented in the inner precincts of the Western world.
>
> In a remarkable turnabout, the former slavers were enfranchised and lifted to a position of real political power vis-à-vis their former masters. And the new national purpose was expressed in the ratification of the Fourteenth and Fifteenth Amendments and passage of the most stringent civil rights legislation ever enacted in America.

It was in this climate that black and white men made the first and, in many ways, the last real attempt to establish an interracial democracy in America. During the heyday of Reconstruction, in the years between 1867 and 1877, black men were elected to the legislatures of every southern state. Lieutenant governors and other cabinet officers were elected in Mississippi, Louisiana, and South Carolina. Twenty black men were sent to the U. S. House of Representatives from the South, and two black politicians were elected to the U. S. Senate from the state of Mississippi.

Reconstruction in all its various facets was a supreme lesson for America, the reading of which might still mark a turning point in our history. As a matter of fact an understanding of the triumphs and failures of this first Reconstruction is indispensable for an understanding of the triumphs and failures of the second Reconstruction we are now undergoing.

New institutions for learning were erected. The black church came into its own as an institution that served many purposes, the spiritual welfare of the people being only one of them. The white churches, mainly in the north, became interested in black education. A large number of college-bred white women from the New England states went to the South to teach in the schools that had been hurriedly established for the newly freed blacks. These women were referred to as New England School Moms. Their contributions to the education of black people in the South during the latter half of the nineteenth century were invaluable.

With support from the federal government, the former slaves became a major factor in Southern political life. Some of them were superintendents of education, state treasurers, adjutant generals, solicitors, judges, and major generals of the state militia. An interracial board was running the University of South Carolina where a black professor, Richard T. Greener, was teaching white and black youth metaphysics and logic.

This interracial goodwill did not last. By 1870 the south regained some of its political strength and was making itself felt in national politics. The tide began to turn against the blacks in the South and the rest of the nation.

The Reconstruction period came to an end soon after the disputed election of 1876 in which the Democratic candidate Samuel J. Tilden seemed to have won the party's first Presidential election since 1856. A recounting of the votes gave the election to Rutherford B. Hayes. This was a foul election. Both Democrats and the Republicans had padded the returns. Both were guilty of using intimidation and violence in preventing large numbers of blacks from voting.

Democrats agreed to the election of Rutherford B. Hayes in return for the promise to withdraw the last federal troops from the South. In April, 1877, white control was restored in the South. The Reconstruction had been betrayed.

The betrayal of the Reconstruction caused massive dislocation and confusion among black people in the South and in the country in general. They were not prepared for this at all. Suddenly many whites whom they had thought of as friends were open and declared enemies. The Freedmen's Bureau and other agencies that had been set up to assist the former slaves were dismantled. Some southern politicians actually attempted to reestablish slavery.

Southern writers, teachers, and bigoted agitators turned the cause of southern redemption into a religion. Finally the Republican party bargained away the political rights of the southern blacks in order to pacify the brooding southern whites. Black politicians held on for a few more years, but their heyday in southern politics was over.

The Southerners were given the right to handle "the Negro" as they saw fit. This "right" opened the door for the rise of the Ku Klux Klan and other bigoted white terrorist organizations. The murder and harassment of blacks by the Ku Klux Klan in the rural areas of the South drove blacks in large numbers to the developing urban southern cities. In the cities the blacks met new trouble that was more complicated. In addition to a new, more sophisticated kind of harassment, they could not find jobs in keeping with their skills, housing was poor, and the right to vote and hold public office had been challenged by the Ku Klux Klan in the cities. The black man's northern white friends deserted him. Many of the New England School Moms who had come into the South a decade earlier had married Southerners and had become southern in their attitude toward the blacks. The new black educational institutions in the South were in serious financial trouble. A unique kind of protracted begging by the heads of these institutions kept most of them alive. This combination of events caused a large number of blacks to migrate from the rural and urban areas of the South to the industrial cities of the North.

These migrating blacks were searching for better jobs and housing, better education for their children—in general a better way of life. Education was the great panacea, and it was pursued as though it would cover all things. Education was what blacks looked for in the leaders. Finally a leader whose life epitomized all of this appeared. His name was Booker T. Washington. The Booker T. Washington era brought black Americans into the twentieth century and started the debate over "what manner of education for black people" that has still not been resolved.

This situation cannot be understood without some reference to its background. The aftereffects of the betrayal of the Reconstruction were still being actually felt throughout black America. The white "friends" that we had in Congress and in the Senate were no longer effective. The Black Reconstruction politicians had been literally driven from public life. During the 1880's Afro-Americans were still voting in the South, but in smaller numbers year after year. The physical segregation that would come later in fact and in law had not developed into a codified system. However, the division of the whites by the Populist movement of the early nineties, and the past Reconstruction threat of political power for the blacks, drove the white conservatives (who had been moderate on the race question) into an extreme political camp. They now became overt racists.

The ground had already been broken and the seeds of protracted tragedy for black Americans had been planted. Even before the rise of Populism in 1890, Mississippi had already adopted several devices—notably the "understanding clause"—to disfranchise black voters. Before being permitted to vote, blacks were asked questions about their understanding of the state's constitution and the Constitution of the United States that were sometimes downright ludicrous and at other times so complicated that the members of the Supreme Court would have had difficulty in answering them.

The annual rate of lynching reached 235 in 1892 and did not drop below at least one hundred per year until 1902. The agricultural depression that began in 1893 reduced a large number of farmers, both black and white, to virtual peonage. It was as C. Vann Woodward observed in his book, *The Strange Career of Jim Crow,* a time of growing pessimism, mounting tension, and unleashed phobias.

In the midst of these trying circumstances, a black educator, Booker T. Washington, was invited to give the keynote address before a biracial audience gathered for the opening of the 1895 Atlanta Cotton States and International Exposition. Mr. Washington's assessment of the situation was that it gave him an opportunity to project some ideas that might lay the basis for goodwill between black and white people in the South. He was aware of the fact that he was the first black American to be invited to address such a large group of white Southerners. He decided to be "perfectly frank and honest"; he decided also "not to say anything that would give undue offense to the South." From the outset his task was prodigious and may well have been impossible.

In the pamphlet, *Black in America: Then and Now* (1969), the Afro-American historian, Edgar A. Tappin, writes a capsule history of the occasion in this manner:

> In all the things that are purely social we can be as separate as the fingers, said the orator, flinging his outstretched hand above his head, "yet one as the hand [arm still aloft but fingers clenched in a fist] in all things essential to mutual progress." With that, according to the dispatch filed from Atlanta, Georgia, on September 18, 1895, by the New York *World* correspondent, James Creelman, "the whole audience was on its feet in delirium of applause."
>
> This was the keynote of a speech that was to have, for several decades, a decisive impact on the relations of blacks and whites in America. The speaker was Booker T. Washington, and this was, Creelman noted, the first time a Negro had made a speech in the south on any important occasion before an audience composed of white men and women.
>
> Some forty thousand visitors had jammed Atlanta for the opening of the important Cotton States and International Exposition. The only black speaker at the opening ceremonies in the great Exposition Building was Washington, who was founder and head of Tuskegee Institute in Alabama. Creelman dsecribed him as being "tall, bony, straight as a Sioux chief" with "high forehead, straight nose, heavy jaws . . . piercing eyes and a commanding manner."
>
> When Washington first took the platform, the blacks sitting in the balcony cheered, but little applause came from the whites on the main floor of the hall. But before he was halfway through his 20-minute speech, Creelman reported, "The multitude was in an uproar of enthusiasm. Handkerchiefs were waved, canes were flourished, hats were tossed in the air. The fairest women of Georgia stood

up and cheered. It was as if the orator had bewitched them." Yet, while the whites burst into wild cheering over Washington's statement about being as separate as the fingers, "most of the Negroes in the audience," Creelman commented, "were crying, perhaps without knowing just why."

In his autobiography, *Up from Slavery* (1901) Washington recalled: "The first thing that I remember, after I had finished speaking was that (former) Governor (Rufus) Bullock rushed across the platform and took me by the hand." Creelman stated that "another shout greeted this demonstration, and for a few minutes the two men stood facing each other, hand in hand." The next day as Washington tried to walk through the streets of Atlanta, crowds of whites surrounded him and "wished to shake his hands," so embarrassing him that he returned to Tuskegee.

The ripple from his speech spread. Telegraphing his impressions to a New York newspaper, Clark Howell, editor-publisher of the Atlanta *Constitution,* described it as "one of the most notable speeches, both as to character and as to the warmth of its reception, ever delivered to a Southern audience."

Newspapers all over the nation published the speech in full and ran editorials commending it. The Boston *Transcript* editorialized that Washington's speech "seems to have dwarfed all other proceedings and the Exposition itself. The sensation that it caused in the press has never been equaled."

President Grover Cleveland wrote Booker T. Washington and thanked him for the copy of the speech that he had sent as a courtesy. After the speech, referred to as "the Atlanta compromise speech," the white press literally anointed Booker T. Washington and made him the spokesman for black America for the next two decades.

Finally Frederick Douglass, who had been the unchallenged leader of black Americans during the latter half of the nineteenth century, passed away on February 20, 1895, six months before Washington's Atlanta speech. With the emergence of Booker T. Washington, a new black leadership class came into being. Some of that class supported Booker T. Washington and some opposed him. How they handled the problems of education still affects the lives of black Americans.

For at least fifty years of his life Frederick Douglass had urged his people never to relinquish their agitation for total freedom. He implored them to constantly seek the ballot box, and cartridge box, upon which liberty depended. He contended: "If there is no struggle there is no progress—power concedes nothing without a demand." He went further to point out that those who sought progress without agitation wanted "crops without plowing—rain without thunder and lightning—the ocean without the awful roar of its mighty waters."

In his book, Professor Tappin reminds us that, until Washington, the dominant theme in black leadership had been militancy. There were always some who counseled submission, caution, and accommodation, but not until his era was this approach clearly in the ascendancy.

The beginning of the "Booker T. Washington era" did not go unnoticed by the ordinary working black people of the South. They too, debated the pros and cons of this new approach to the position of black people in this country. And like the black intellectuals they also were divided. The migration from the South that had started soon after the betrayal of Reconstruction was continued. The white South had regained its political strength and was using it. So far as they were concerned the wounds of the Civil War had nearly healed, and the South was firmly back in the Union. Union and Confederate veterans now made a ceremony out of the "burying of the hatchet," forgiving and forgetting the past. But in matters relating to the black Americans this attitude of reconciliation did not prevail. Southerners had been systematically taking away the rights of black people year after year, while the rest of the country looked away, pretending they did not know what was happening, thereby silently agreeing with the action of the South.

This situation did not develop suddenly, for two decades it had been in the making. In the Civil Rights cases of 1883, the court had declared unconstitutional the Civil Rights Act of 1875, which required for all races "the full equal enjoyment of accommodations in inns, theaters . . . and public conveyances on land and water." Then in 1896 (a year after Booker T. Washington made his Atlanta speech), in the case of *Plessy v. Ferguson,* the court upheld a Louisiana law requiring all railway companies to provide "equal but separate accommodations for the white and colored races." This law extended to education, thus the supposedly separate but equal schools. Now, many blacks who were migrating from the South were also searching for a better education for their children. This migration, and others that followed, made the black urban ghettos of the North. Harlem was, and still is, the best known of all the northern urban ghettos. This community was in the making long before the migrations started.

Harlem has been called, and may well be, the cultural and intellectual capital of the black race in the Western world. It has also been called other names, less complimentary—names like "a cancer in the heart of a city" and "a large-scale laboratory experiment in the race problem." Some of the most colorful and dynamic personalities in the black world have used Harlem as a vantage point, a platform and proving ground for their ideas and ambitions. The "Back to Africa" movement and the more vocal aspects of Black Nationalism found a greater acceptance in Harlem than in any other place. This cannot be understood without some knowledge of how and why Harlem came into being in the first place.

Sometime in 1626 in a Dutch outpost called New Amster

dam, now New York City, eleven Africans were imported and assigned quarters on the fringe of what is now the Bowery. Those black laborers eventually built a wagon road to a place in the upper part of the settlement that the Dutch called "Haarlem." About 274 years passed before Harlem (now spelled with one "a") was changed into a black metropolis.

Eighteen years after their arrival the eleven Africans petitioned the Dutch authorities with the support of the rank-and-file colonists and were finally granted their freedom. The liberated men, who now had wives, settled in a swamp known today as Greenwich Village. They built this swamp into a prosperous community and attracted other settlers.

The peaceful relations between Africans and the white settlers came to an end when the British gained control of New Amsterdam in 1664 and introduced chattel slavery.

In 1741 an African named Caesar led the first slave uprising in New York and in 1799, more than a half century before Lincoln's proclamation, a bill was passed in New York beginning the gradual emancipation of slaves.

Black slaves fought in the American Revolution in large numbers; some of them fought as replacements for their white masters who did not choose to fight.

The first independent act of these slaves after the end of slavery in the North was to break away from the Methodist Episcopal Church and start the African Methodist Episcopal Zion Church. After the Civil War these former slaves moved further uptown in the settlement that was going to be New York City, but they were a long way from Harlem.

The mass exodus and settlement of black Americans in Harlem started in 1900 after New York's disastrous race riot. One of the spiritual leaders of the movement to Harlem was the Reverend Adam Clayton Powell, Sr., father of the late former Congressman. The Harlem that blacks began to move into in large numbers around 1900 was a cheerful neighbor-

hood of broad streets, brownstone dwellings, and large apart-
ment houses. Thoroughbred horses were seen on Lenox
Avenue, and polo was actually being played at the polo
grounds.

There were several migrations to Harlem, but the migration from the South was the most notable. Many blacks who
had been residents of New York City for generations began
to move farther uptown before the end of the nineteenth
century. These blacks were being pursued by new emigrants
from Europe who were moving into the scattered black communities in downtown New York City that had been in
existence for over two hundred years.

Harlem's new settlers began to build institutions. Old
downtown institutions and churches were brought uptown.
The community took on a new character. In many ways it
became more than a community. It became a frame of mind
with international importance. It became the headquarters
of cults, self-proclaimed kings, messiahs and pretenders. In a
more serious vein it became the intellectual and spiritual
home of African people in the Western world. Some of the
most important men and movements in America's black urban ghettos would develop in Harlem.

With the spread of lynching and the lack of job opportunities, the migration from the South continued. The new
settlers were looking for a better way of life for themselves
and their children. They wanted better jobs and the right
to vote and to influence the political leaders of their community. For their children they wanted good schools with
teachers who would develop their potential. Through their
children they saw a future that was much brighter than anything that they had dreamed of for themselves.

While the settlement of the Harlem community was in its
formative stages, other black communities in Detroit, Chicago, Boston, and Philadelphia were expanding to accommodate the new migrants from the South.

As the country moved into the twentieth century the debate over what was a relevant education for black Americans continued. Most of the debate was centered around the educational program of Booker T. Washington and what would later be called "The Tuskegee Machine."

In the book, *Black in America: Then and Now,* Professor Tappin explains the essence of the Booker T. Washington program in this manner:

> Washington took ignorant, backward blacks living in abysmal poverty as cotton sharecroppers and taught them how to improve their lives by cleanliness, industry, thrift, diversified farming, family budgeting and better planning. Tuskegee was practicing community involvement, uplifting agricultural extension work, and home demonstration techniques long before the terms were invented or the Smith-Level Act passed.
>
> Hired by Washington, the great agricultural scientist George Washington Carver was on the Tuskegee faculty from 1896 to 1943, enrichening the South and benefiting white and black southerners by his discoveries. From 1881 to 1915 Washington headed and lived at Tuskegee Institute, learning to get along with and gaining the support of whites in the deep south. Understandably his approach to race relations would differ from Douglass' approach.
>
> The downturn in the black man's fortunes in the last quarter of the nineteenth century also affected Washington's outlook. He became convinced that agitation and militancy were useless in the face of a determined drive by northern and southern whites to reduce blacks to a degraded second-class status.
>
> He believed that withdrawal from politics would ease tensions and give blacks a chance to strengthen black communities by economic success as black craftsmen, businessmen, and professionals for a subsequent rise to first class citizenship. The increasing racism and drift toward disenfranchisement convinced him that submission and accommodation were the best tactics for the times.

Institutional racism with its roots in the nineteenth century had already become an obstacle to the education of black Americans in both the North and South. Ideas of racial superiority were intensified and a whole body of "scientific" literature was produced to support this attitude.

Professor William Graham Sumner of Yale University pointed out that evolution "instead of supporting the natural equality of man, would give a demonstration of their unequality." Further he attacked the Congressional Reconstruction laws that tried to legislate political equality between blacks and whites.

Late nineteenth-century imperialism and the Kipling concept of "taking up the white man's burden" gave support to American racism. The United States had now acquired overseas colonies. The rationale for ruling over these people was not much different from the rationale for denying full citizenship to black Americans. The northern politicians and social reformers who had been the defenders of the rights of blacks were silent. The editor of the *Atlantic Monthly* noted: "If the stronger and cleverer race is free to impose its will upon new-caught sullen peoples on the other side of the globe, why not in South Carolina and Mississippi?"

Booker T. Washington never took a public stand against the rising tide of Jim Crow, lynchings, and the mass disenfranchisement of black voters. In the Atlanta Cotton Exposition speech he had asserted that the leaders of his people had shown poor judgment in beginning at the political top as freedmen rather than at the bottom of life working up by proving to be substantial citizens. He said, "Agitation of questions of social equality is the extreme folly" because an "opportunity to earn a dollar in a factory just now is worth indefinitely more than the opportunity to spend a dollar in an opera house."

The words of Booker T. Washington's Atlanta speech were still reechoing early in the century when an anti-Booker T.

Washington school of thought was developed and led by W. E. B. Du Bois.

Professor Tappin puts this conflict in perspective in his book, *Black in America: Then and Now.* He said:

> Not only presidents, but governors, congressmen, and philanthropists consulted Washington before making any appointments of, or donations to, blacks. He served on the boards of the major foundations concerned with black education—the Slater, Phelps Stokes and Jeanes Funds.
>
> After a time, Du Bois explained, "almost no Negro institution could collect funds without the recommendation or acquiescence of Mr. Washington." To displease him could dry up funds vital to a black college's survival.
>
> Du Bois further charged that Northern capitalists wanted a large force of trained blacks as a counterweight to union demands and the thrust of white workers for wage increases. Black liberal arts colleges might disrupt such plans. Washington's philosophy of industrial education fitted in so well with the plans of these capitalists that they "proposed by building up his prestige and power to control the Negro group," charged Du Bois. "The Negro intelligentsia was to be suppressed and hammered into conformity."
>
> Washington's Tuskegee Machine influenced black newspapers and magazines. The Tuskegee news bureau, directed by Emmett J. Scott, sent out a flood of news releases and canned editorials. By placing or withholding ads, the well-endowed Tuskegee clique persuaded many black editors, most of whose publications were in financial straits, to carry these materials favorable to Washington's views. Moreover the Tuskegee cabal secretly purchased several black periodicals, controlling them unbeknownst to the public.
>
> Du Bois, the leading foe of this "Tuskegee Machine" was born in 1868 in Great Barrington, Mass., a town of 5,000, with only 50 black residents. He was the top student in the town's high school. Educated at Fisk and Harvard

Universities and in Germany, he received his Ph.D. degree from Harvard in 1895. Published in 1896, his dissertation, "Suppression of the African Slave Trade to the United States," became the first volume in the Harvard Historical Studies.

Sensitive to the racial rebuffs he experienced despite his brilliant record, Du Bois became aloof and antagonistic. He taught at Wilberforce University for two years and spent a year making a pioneering sociological study published as "The Philadelphia Negro" (1899). From 1897 to 1910, he taught sociology at Atlanta University. His eventual opposition to Booker T. Washington imperiled the school, but its white president, Horace Humstead, stood by him.

Until 1903, Du Bois did not challenge Washington's Atlanta compromise. An admirer of Frederick Douglass, he viewed Washington as sharing Douglass's long-range goals even though employing moderate tactics. But Du Bois became increasingly irritated at the Tuskegee Machine, recalling that "above all I resent the choking off of even mild and reasonable opposition to Mr. Washington in both the Negro press and the white."

After the "Boston riot," Du Bois became the active leader of the radical blacks. William Monroe Trotter (1872–1934), brilliant, Harvard-educated editor-founder of the Boston *Guardian,* heckled Washington when the latter addressed a rally in Boston in July 1903. Tuskegeeans had Mr. Trotter arrested for provoking these disturbances. Subsequently they tried to get his partner fired from the Boston library post.

Du Bois had taken on the Tuskegeeans that spring in an essay, "Of Me: Booker T. Washington and others." In his book, "The Souls of Black Folks" (1903), Du Bois denounced "the hushing of the criticism of honest opponents. . . ." Pointing to the setbacks resulting from Washington's temporary abandonment of black political power, civil rights, and higher education, Du Bois's essay asked rhetorically, "Can (blacks) make effective progress in economic lines if they are deprived of political rights, made a servile caste, and allowed only the most meager chance for developing their exceptional man?" Du Bois's answer was "an emphatic no."

Du Bois resented Washington's emphasis on training blacks in craft skills, some already obsolete, the neglect of liberally educating the "talented tenth," the gifted elite that Du Bois felt would lead the race forward. Du Bois also contended that Washington "counsels a silent submission to civil inferiority such as is bound to sap the manhood to any race . . ."

Thus Du Bois made three demands: (1) "the right to vote," (2) "civil activity," and (3) "the education of youth according to ability."

These basic demands formed the nucleus of the declaration of principles adopted by the 30 black men who met at the first Niagara Conference in July, 1905, at Niagara, Canada. Du Bois and Trotter (Monroe Trotter) called the meeting and drafted the declaration . . . The Niagara Movement was the first national organization of militant blacks, but its financial status was precarious. The "Tuskegee Machine" infiltrated spies, blocked news coverage, and inspired editorials assailing these radicals.

At the base of the conflict was the still unanswered question, "What kind of education is most relevant for black Americans?"

The black American had entered the twentieth century searching for new directions, politically, culturally, and institutionally. The black woman was very much a part of this search. Booker T. Washington's Atlanta Cotton Exposition Address (1895) had set in motion a great debate among black people about their direction and their place in the developing American social order. The black woman was very much a part of the debate. New men and movements were emerging. Some men, principally Bishop Henry McNeal Turner, were questioning whether black people had any future in America. The black woman answered this question in the affirmative by pouring massive energy into building of new institutions, mainly schools.

In the field of education the black woman's creative contribution had a lasting effect that is still apparent. Some of the most outstanding of these women during the first half of the twentieth century are: Fanny Jackson Coppin, Maria L. Baldwin, Lucy Laney, Charlotte Hawkins Brown, Mary McLeod Bethune, Maudelle Brown Bousfield, and Nannie Helen Burroughs.

Black Americans came into the twentieth century with some of the unresolved educational problems of the nineteenth century. Carter G. Woodson called attention to this in two near-classic, though still sadly neglected, books: *The Education of the Negro Prior to 1861* (1919), and *The Mis-Education of the Negro"* (1938).

Dr. Woodson tells us, "It required little argument to convince intelligent masters that slaves, who had some conception of modern civilization and understood the language of their owners, would be more valuable than rude men with whom one could not communicate. The question, however, as to exactly what kind of training these Negroes should have and how far it should go, was to the white race then as much a matter of perplexity as it is now."

The decision among the slave owners who agreed on an education at all for their slaves was that the slave would receive only the kind of education that benefited the slave master by making the slave a more productive worker on the plantation. From the beginning the black Americans were educated to serve others and not themselves. In *The Education of the Negro Prior to 1861,* Dr. Woodson outlines the beginning of black education in this country.

> The history of the education of the ante-bellum Negroes, therefore, falls into two periods. The first extends from

the time of the introduction of slavery to the climax of the insurrectionary movement about 1835, when the majority of the people in this country answered in the affirmative the question whether or not it was prudent to educate their slaves. Then followed the second period, when the industrial revolution changed slavery from a patriarchal to an economic institution, and when intelligent Negroes, encouraged by abolitionists, made so many attempts to organize servile insurrections that the pendulum began to swing the other way. By this time most southern white people reached the conclusion that it was impossible to cultivate the mind of Negroes without arousing overmuch self-assertion.

The early advocates of the education of Negroes were of three classes: first, masters who desired to increase the economic efficiency of their labor supply; second, sympathetic persons who wished to help the oppressed; and third, zealous missionaries who, believing that the message of divine love came equally to all, taught slaves the English language that they might learn the principles of the Christian religion. Through the kindness of the first class, slaves had their best chance for mental improvement. Each slaveholder dealt with the situation to suit himself, regardless of public opinion. Later when measures were passed to prohibit the education of slaves, some masters, always a law unto themselves, continued to teach their Negroes in defiance of the hostile legislation. Sympathetic persons were not able to accomplish much because they were usually reformers, who not only did not own slaves, but dwelt in practically free settlement far from the plantations on which the bondmen lived.

The Spanish and French missionaries had a different approach to the education of the slaves. Some of them were anxious to see the Africans enlightened and brought into the church. This was a change from their previous position when they had originally advocated the enslavement of the Africans rather than the Indians.

The position of these Catholic missionaries forced the English into a more positive stance in matters relating to the education of the Africans. Dr. Woodson tells us, "The English were put to shame by the noble example of the Catholics. They had to find a way to overcome the objections of these who, granting that the enlightment of the slaves might not lead to servile insurrection, nevertheless feared that their conversion might work manumission. This situation forced the English to deal with a contradiction within the Christian church that still exists. Can a Christian hold another Christian as a slave and still be a Christian? In order to deal with the urgency of this matter the colonists secured, through legislation by their assemblies and formal declaration of the Bishop of London, the abrogation of the law that a Christian could not be held as a slave. After being allowed access to the church of England, and sent out by the Society for the Propagation of the Gospel among the Heathen in Foreign Parts, the colonists undertook to educate the slaves for the purpose of extensive proselytizing.

Reaction to this plan was not slow in coming. During the first quarter of the nineteenth century, especially in the South, reactionaries forced public opinion to gradually prohibit the education of Africans, except in some urban communities where progressive blacks were able to provide their own schools. The massive slave revolts that came during this period convinced a large number of whites, some of them former allies of the blacks, that educating blacks was a dangerous thing. This opinion continued until after the Civil War when blacks began to build new institutions, mainly schools. Most of these new schools soon began to fall into old traps. They were imitations of white schools, whose teachings were offensive to black people. Now the education of Afro-Americans began to move on several levels. Education in churches, community centers, and in homes began to supplement the education in the schools. In these independent institutions, lay historians began the formal search for the African Heritage.

In what can still be referred to as "The Booker T. Washington Era (1895–1915)," new men and movements were emerging. The Niagara Movement, under the leadership of W. E. B. Du Bois and Monroe Trotter, was born in 1905. Some of the ideas of the Niagara Movement went into the making of the NAACP, in 1909.

During the years leading to the eve of the First World War and those that immediately followed, the flight from the South continued. Over a half million blacks migrated northward in search of better paying wartime jobs, better schools for their children, and better housing. For a short while they entertained the illusion that they had been improved and that they had escaped from the oppression of the South. The illusion was short-lived. Race riots in wartime (East St. Louis, 1917) and in postwar time (Chicago, 1919) awakened the new urban settlers to reality. In Washington, D.C., President Woodrow Wilson and the southern Democrats who had come to power with him had introduced segregation in federal facilities, which had long been integrated. Booker T. Washington had died in 1915. An investigation into his last years revealed he had privately battled against disenfranchisement and had secretly financed law suits against segregation, but publicly he maintained his submissive stance. With Washington gone and the influence of the "Tuskegee Machine" in decline, a new class of black radicals came forward. As founder-editor of the NAACP's *Crisis* magazine, Du Bois urged in 1918, "Let us, while this war lasts, forget our special grievances and close ranks shoulder to shoulder with our fellow citizens . . ." The continued discrimination against black Americans, both soldiers and civilians, soon made W. E. B. Du Bois regret having made this statement. The end of the war brought no improvement to the lives of black Americans. The then prevailing condition made a large number of them ripe for the militant program of Marcus Garvey. This was the beginning of the heroic and troubled years of the black urban ghetto.

In the years between wars, the black urban ghetto grew larger while the schools and education in general deteriorated. The migrations from the South continued and pride kept a lot of black Americans from returning to the South and admitting that their sojourn in the North in search of a better way of life for themselves and their children had failed.

The black communities of the North became urban colonies. The first thing that was colonized was the educational systems within those communities. Most of the teachers were white. They had no deep feelings of understanding for the community or the people. The seeds of the present day crisis in urban education had been planted.

3

A Master Plan for Urban Education: The 1970 Urban Education Task Force

by Wilson C. Riles

Wilson Riles was born in rural Louisiana, near Alexandria, on June 27, 1917. He was orphaned at an early age, worked his way through junior and senior high school, and followed his stepparents to Arizona, where he entered Arizona State College.

After receiving his B.A. and M.A. degrees at Arizona State College, and serving three years in the Army Air Corps, he began his education career as a teacher in a one-room school house on an Apache Indian reservation. He became a school principal in the Arizona schools before moving to Los Angeles to work with the interfaith Fellowship of Reconciliation. He joined the California State Department of Education in 1958 as a consultant in minority hiring, and was later able to establish California's compensatory education program as a model for the nation. In 1969, he was appointed chairman of the Nixon Administration's Task Force on Urban Education.

In 1970, he was elected California's State Superintendent of Public Instruction, a position responsible for the education of 4.5 million children.

Two topics that seemed to draw problems like magnets during the sixties were urbanism and education. To combine the two and tackle them with a task force was a feat few cherished but one which the late Assistant Secretary/Commissioner of Education-designate James E. Allen, Jr., took on during the early months of the Nixon Administration in 1969.

Nine months later the task force report was on the desks of the administration. It was not too warmly received. Among other things it recommended money, lots of money, and a perseverance that a country under the press of a war budget and a recession was not ready to take on.

This did not diminish the merit of the report, nor the very live message its substance will carry for some time to come.

The task force—with its fifty-nine cross-country, top-talent members—concluded that urban education should be the administration's top domestic priority. It recommended an omnibus Urban Education Act that would create a bureau of urban education in the U. S. Office of Education and give that bureau up to $14.5 billion to spend. The money would be spent in new and fresh ways, reordering much of the old along the lines of greater local control and relevance, prudent planning, and hope.

That inquiry began with an identification of problems. It was readily apparent—from newspapers, from tax records, from summaries of contemporary literature and studies—that urban education had less money to meet greater problems than most other areas of education.

Not quite as apparent, but still as consistent, was that in the midst of all these problems there remained this promise: that with careful planning and effective administration, education for the urban individual was still his best hope for a one-generation-up-and-out triumph over his plight.

The key, then, was to maximize the planning, make more effective the organization and administration and increase the number of individuals for whom this promise comes true.

Matching the promise to fact had to account for the sheer

enormity of the problem. Facing this magnitude, the task force decided that any profound, long-range solution must rely in the main on change within the current public education structure, not on stimulus or activity outside of the structure. This did not preclude the important role filled by "alternative education," but it did not make that role a fulcrum. The vastness of the problem could be met only by the vastness of the broad public system.

The task force was struck almost immediately with the absence of form and flow in current urban education attempts. Most often learning is islanded off from the community behind a set of walls and a system of bells, with classifications by age and with dramatic beginning and ending points for each school day and each school life.

Corrective attempts are remedial, not preventive, and are really spot-checks, mere patches on a very complex quilt.

A realistic definition of education would show that learning is going on at all times and in every corner of the neighborhood, and any formal learning process should take this into account. As a minimum, the report says, conventional curricula must be infused with new topics such as maintenance of individuality and the problems of noise, overcrowding, and narcotics addiction.

But better, the curriculum should be expanded to encompass the very processes of the community itself, and the school should draw upon the supportive services—health, employment, recreation—of the community as well.

Nor should education follow the age-old assumptions of age itself. Educational planning should acquire a certain design and consistency from preschool through higher education and on into the upper adult years as well. Life and learning should be synonymous and progress should be by need, not by birthday.

Thus the program should be a package, not patches; dynamic, not static; relevant, not obtuse; and it should have a cohesiveness and a flow that give it some sense of direction on its own and natural integration with the community.

The task force found major violations of these principles of program design almost everywhere it looked.

Similarly, in program content the task force found severe deficiencies. The curriculum most often has been developed for the suburbs and has little to say to the inner-city child.

"Most of the programs have been conceived from a perspective that implicitly compares the inner-city student from a minority group with a white, middle-class age and grade-level suburban counterpart," the report says. "The results are inevitably negative—the inner-city student winds up being described as deficient in verbal ability, reading achievement, marketable economic skills and social skills. . . . Consequently, most of the programs are designed from a negative standpoint, namely, overcoming deficiencies, and are almost never designed from the positive view of capitalizing on strengths."

Those strengths of the inner-city student, the report points out, are "his pride, his tough pragmatic problem-solving, his resiliency in the face of daily economic uncertainties, his personal loyalty to his group, his sense of humor, his candor— or lack of hypocrisy."

In fact, the report says, many current systems have trouble perceiving just who their students are. "Possessing essentially the same general goals as previous waves of immigrants (e.g., economic security, self-respect, personal safety), the minorities today nevertheless manifest some differences in values, needs and problems. These, the system's often unrecognized biases and unchanging expectations, have often limited the system's capacity to teach effectively children who do not have the same expectations, such as being oriented to middle-class values and expectations, being 'ready' for reading, and having the structural orientation that facilitates shifting from subject matter to subject matter as dictated by time blocs rather than by interest and substance. The failure of many teachers to perceive their students as they are stems from complex origins relating to the status assigned by society to teaching the disadvantaged and the levels of competency and experience of the teachers."

This failure in perception is among the causes for a revolt by one corner of the school's constituency: its students. They drop out or fail to achieve or resort to violence.

Another constituency, when it detects failure, refuses to pass bond issues; or it quits coming to board meetings; or it comes to board meetings in angry droves, demanding a dismantlement of the school system itself. This constituency is the community.

The community might be less likely to arrive at a verdict of failure if it had participated in the decisions that led to the current situation. For that matter, there might have been less failure. But the communities have been largely excluded, and school boards, administrators, and teacher organizations have not always met community needs.

Hence the very pressing and constant pressure to decentralize and dismantle, or at the very least to put the community into one of three relationships with the system: as participants, as partners, or as controllers.

The task force clearly sided with the source and reasons for this pressure. "Regardless of the particular form which community involvement takes, this role must include policy-making in the areas of: (1) priorities for spending the available monies; (2) design of curriculum and implementation of program components; and (3) employment and evaluation of key personnel."

Part of the failure to meet needs, and of the resulting community revolt, is that the inner-city community has been made up of the emerging minorities, and the school governing structure has not. The task force again sided with the political push and pull to correct this situation: "We also believe that the current thrust composed of separatism, local community control of schools and insistence on the recognition of minority identities (e.g., black history, La Raza) by various groups is the all-too-logical result of the basic lack of commitment and the slowness of action to achieve integration. The quality, recognition and acceptance which were to have occurred with earlier thrusts on integration, such as equal employment opportunity, fair housing and school desegregation, have not really materialized. We suggest that the composite thrust of separatism, local community control and the demand for a recognized identity are not over the long term antithetical to the aims of integration. Rather, it constitutes an attempt to achieve through other channels what earlier thrusts have only partially fulfilled."

The task force writers further drive home the fact that this type of separatism is not necessarily negative in texture: ". . . it reflects neither the primary reliance of the minorities on public-spirited members of the white majority to do something for them nor the 'we'll go it alone' stance of certain groups within the minorities. Instead, other groups within these minorities are actively seeking legitimate power bases or positions of strength from which they can negotiate as equals with the majority. In striving to achieve this negotiating capability, the minorities are developing a new thrust in the continuing struggle for genuine integration which could be termed interdependency. As emerging here, it is saying, 'You need us every bit as much as we need you—so we better find ways to cooperate as equal partners in our mutual concerns. It is only by working together that we are going to solve our society's problems.' This emergent—and newest—thrust seems to hold potentially the greatest promise for achieving genuine integration since it concomitantly recognizes common goals (e.g., economic self-sufficiency, a healthful environment, improved educational programs) and proposes to work cooperatively on the ways to achieve them."

Thus, "We strongly support a broadened view of racial and ethnic integration which includes within it those actions which superficially and over the short term may seem militant."

Integration itself, the task force felt, should be part and parcel of the program, not something tagged on or superimposed over the existing structure. It should be designed into the program in a natural and positive way, in a way that enhances education, not in a way that disrupts it. But it should be a part of every program, a major part.

Another element regularly missing from urban education systems is a set of performance standards with a follow-up assessment guide, the task force found. Performance criteria, they felt, should state in clear terms what the student should be expected to be able to do, the "knowledges, attitudes and skills which the students themselves are expected to demonstrate . . . in terms of overt behaviors."

Assessment should be a major consideration, beginning with the planning phase, not footnoted to the program later. It should be a self-evolving, self-tightening procedure whose major aim is to assist the teacher and the individual student, not pit school against school in academic sparring matches. Moreover, performance and assessment criteria should be set for all school staffs, beginning with the top office, and the criteria should be broadly derived, beginning with the community.

Finally, in the matter of money, the task force found the source of much aggravation. The cities have been abandoned by the high tax producers and invaded by the high tax consumers. Public support for schools at the polls has dwindled in the cities as well as in the suburbs, with construction bonds and tax overrides regularly going down. Private schools, often concentrated in the cities, are closing down under the pressure of high costs, spurring the public school enrollment and the need for new plants. City costs are higher

than suburban costs, not only because maintenance, vandal-
ism, and wages are higher, but also because the very nature
of the challenge—to lift a child out of poverty and a low
educational environment—is greater.

The states' answers, for historical and political reasons,
have been to skew state aid formulas against the cities. The
formulas were laid during a time when the cities were rich
and the nonurban areas were poor, and so the formulas
favored the latter. A 1962 study shows that of the thirty-seven
large city areas studies, the central cities received larger educational aid per pupil in only eight cases, while the outside
areas received larger educational aid per pupil in the pre-
ponderant twenty-nine cases. With reapportioned state legislatures moving to reflect the swelling suburbs, the prospect
for state aid formulas that are fairer to the cities looks dim.

But a study of state aid reveals even more fundamental
problems. "State and local taxation is notoriously regressive
and highly visible as compared with the federal income tax,"
the report states. "State sales taxes, which are noted as
'pennies for the Governor' with every purchase, and local
property taxes, which have little relationship to ability to
pay, are widely resented and are in some places reaching the
limits of expansion. If needed new support is to be made
available for the support of city schools, the share carried
by Federal revenues will have to be vastly increased."

In fiscal 1969, the burden of primary and secondary school
expenditures was being carried 52 percent by local sources,
40.7 percent by state and 7.3 percent by federal. The task
force took a serious look at the federal role.

"Simply stated, the funding of federal programs has not
assisted hard-pressed urban areas to meet the educational
challenges which confront them," reads the preface to the
report's federal-fund study.

The federal share, to begin with, is too small to have any
really dynamic potential. Even current amounts seem always

in jeopardy, and so administrators are reluctant to assign their best staff to precarious programs. The funds do not come early enough for real planning. When they do come they are in the shape of single purpose programs that don't integrate well with the regular program. The net effect on the disadvantaged child's daily school life has been small.

A partial exception to these conditions has been Title I of the Elementary and Secondary Education Act of 1965, Compensatory Education. That program has presented a package, "a combination of modified curriculum, staff development, enlightened staff attitudes, supportive services, parent support, and adequate funding." And that package is having some positive results.

But even Title I has had restraints. Many local administrators have "spread Title I allocations thinly in order to include as many students as possible. The result is a superficial veneer of fragmented programs or new equipment rather than an integrated, high-impact intervention to achieve major educational change."

In its draft report, the urban education task force's committee on finance and governmental relations said that "the Federal Government does not now have a systematic way of measuring its own overall resource allocation priorities in education." As a partial result, it is pointed out, by astute maneuvers in the art of grantsmanship a wealthy suburb can out-acquire its poorer inner-city neighbor in federal funds, even with the highly concentrated effort of Title I on the inner-city.

The fate of the federal role was uncertain and evolving at the time of the task force report. There was a clear and positive trend to move from specific education efforts into broad social action. This had caused some evaluation maladjustments. Evaluators continued to view the newer programs as solely educational, when really they were social and political. And politically, the redistribution of educational political power to enhance the constituents and the old tussle between research and development and action remained uncertain.

But this uncertainty had an attractive feature. The federal role—less rigid, with greater resources and fewer precedents—was ripe for comment and constructive change, and that is what the task force was all about.

The task force devised a short-range and a long-range set of solutions. The short-range solutions were more predictable, but just as needed.

The short-range recommendations, designed as "holding actions," can best be stated verbatim:

Title I, Elementary and Secondary Education Act
1. Title I must be funded at or near full authorization.
2. States should be encouraged to concentrate funds in areas with high concentrations of disadvantaged populations.
3. Appropriations must be made in advance.
4. A bypass amèndment should be included to directly aid non-public schools when states fail to do so.
5. Health, Education and Welfare audits of local and state administration of Title I funds and other related programs should be made available to the public.

Vocational education
1. Congress should adequately fund all parts of the Vocational Education Amendments of 1968.
2. The Commissioner should concentrate funds under the discretionary parts of the Vocational Education Amendment on the urban disdvantaged.

Research and Development
1. Top priority should be given to the needs of the urban disadvantaged child.
2. Emphasis should be on developing models which could be used in inner-city classrooms across the country.
3. Educational laboratories and research and development centers should focus on urban problems.
4. There should be an effort to involve a broader range of people in the research effort.

Training

1. There should be more effort to bring new kinds of people into the field of education, and to establish early recruitment of such people.
2. The Teacher Corps and the Urban Teacher Corps should be expanded.
3. Changes in certification laws should be encouraged.

Higher education

1. There should be fuller funding of existing programs designed to aid the disadvantaged, such as Upward Bound, Special Services, Talent Search, Equal Opportunity grants, work-study and National Defense Education Act loans.
2. Funds should be made available for one-year federally funded college preparatory programs for the disadvantaged.

Discretionary Funds of the Commissioner

1. Discretionary programs should focus on urban education.
2. New monies should be set aside for planning and instituting urban education programs.

Data on Urban Education Funds

1. Data on the flow of federal funds to the central city school districts in each standard metropolitan statistical area should be published annually.

National commission

1. A National Commission on the Future Financing of American Education should be established.

National advisory council

1. Greater weight should be given to the inclusion of poor people on the council.
2. The council should be given a clear mandate to review all federal programs which affect the lives of the disadvantaged.

Rural areas—While the task force feels that urban needs deserve priority consideration and separate treatment, the needs of rural areas deserve comparable study and consideration.

The real work of the task force went into its long-range solutions. It began with the notion of a master plan that would attack all sides of the urban education question in a synchronized fashion, because anything less would not mend the faults of the current piecemeal approach.

To bring about the master plan, the task force recommended that "the Office of Education immediately establish an Office of Programs Serving the Disadvantaged under an Associate Commissioner, to become the Bureau of Urban Education with broader mandates upon the passage of an Urban Education Act."

The Urban Education Act was to be the midwife of the master plan. The master plan itself was to have mini-master plans, developed by each local urban area to serve its needs. The master plans were to be guided by certain criteria: "a broadened definition of education; the use of existing and heretofore largely unutilized instructional resources; the use of financial resources at all levels of public and private sources; a clearly articulated needs statement indicating a knowledge of the target area and its problems on a need priority basis; a general set of objectives for a total program which will consider those problems of the city which have direct bearing on the process of education; a specific set of educational objectives to be met by the educational program of the master plan; a full description of the program; plans for continuous assessment of the program in terms of student performance; and plans for an evaluation of the overall institutional performance."

The task force also laid out the following survey stakes for these master plans:

Planning: This component should be dynamic and self-evolving. Its phases should be initial design, preliminary implementation, feedback and modification, and it should assume as vital aspects of its process integration and institutional change. The form of integration should not be mandated from above but should be developed from below. "There is no single or simple way of achieving real integration," the report reads. "A community applying for funds should demonstrate how its educational plan contributes to overcoming racial and ethnic isolation." Plans should consider gains for the community as well as for students. A first step in planning is an accurate description of current performance, and the development of this description, paid for with existing local funds, should be a prerequisite to an application for funds.

Personnel development: reform in staff recruitment, training and development should aim toward an understanding of attitudes for working with target populations, process-centered learning, involvement of community residents, supportive services, and utilization of student life experiences.

Curriculum: alternative learning routes leading to student-oriented performance objectives should be included. These routes should cover not only some traditional academic areas, but also areas that help the urban child in particular to cope with urban problems. "Special emphasis should be given to the communication processes, and within these, reading should be stressed because of its significance to educational achievement and employment."

Supportive services: whatever essential services that are necessary for effective learning must be included. These include medical, dental, nutritional, clothing, shelter, social and psychological, counseling and guidance, occupational and educational placement, dropout prevention, personnel recruitment, and recreational.

Community determination: Mechanisms to include all sides of the inner-city community—its residents, its colleges and universities, vocational and technical schools, and private industries and foundations—should be developed.

Experimentation: The master plan can be freckled with pilot or "sub-programs" to try out new techniques and to provide an air of constant enterprise and innovation.

Assessment: Federal funding should be conditioned on the attainment of measurable standards. These objectives should be fair, student-oriented, and integral to the program from its early planning stage.

Facilities: Facilities should blend with the local program, have a favorable impact on the local community and economy and, where possible, have a multipurpose use.

The task force felt that "alternative education" programs outside of or in competition with the master plans "should be funded to meet specific needs and problems not taken into account by the more comprehensive master plan." Among those programs considered were educational parks, publicly funded private schools, city-as-classroom structures, and the voucher system.

In terms of who should run the master plan, the task force envisioned substantial decentralization and community determination as major avenues to institutional change. Decentralization, for programmatic and administrative matters, should reach the individual school level. The task force felt that decentralization and metropolitanism—the move to join the inner-city and the wider metropolitan area through educational programs—were compatible.

The role of the states in the master plan is initially one of self-improvement. State formulas and practices that deprive cities of their fair share of attention must be revised. Federal incentive matching grants might be a way to encourage revision.

States also should establish urban education units in their state education departments; revise certification requirements to permit new sources of personnel; create local units for urban education information dissemination; and design approval mechanisms for urban education proposals. Again, incentive grants can be used.

The funding process should be fluid and flexible, the task force felt. The emphasis should be on economic and performance criteria and on fully funded grants, not on a series of partial grants. Nonpublic school children should be permitted to participate. If state agencies fail to provide sufficient guarantees of efficiency and willingness to perform on behalf of urban areas, legislation should permit bypassing the state agencies.

The muscle of the master plan would necessarily be in the funding itself. In resources—equipment, teachers, planning—the task force saw a need for at least a one-third increase for the urban areas. This resource increase, in turn, would generate an increase in local expenditures of 50 percent over current levels.

The task force's outside figure of money needed by 1975 was $14.5 billion. This included $3.3 billion for cities of 25,000–50,000 population, $3.6 billion for cities of 50,000–100,000 population and $7.5 billion for cities of over 100,000 population. Each population size, beginning with the largest first, was offered as an additional optional funding route.

The task force broke the budget of each category, by city size, down into increments of planning grants, development grants, operational grants, facilities, and training. For cities of 100,000 population and over, for example, planning took $62.8 million and development took $407.4 million in the immediate fiscal years, while by 1975 there would need to be $5.82 billion for operations and $1.45 billion for facilities and $291 million for training.

The task force was deliberately structured to present a diversity of views, and as a result there were several minority reports. For example, in the area of funding a minority felt that only additional federal funds at the rate of $30 million a year over the current amount would be prudent. The funds would be channeled to school districts on a formula basis.

A minority also felt that a federal policy on decentralization and community determination was unnecessary, and they further believed that the federal government had "no appropriate role in the area of recommending criteria and program components" for the master plans.

This diversity of opinion was a source of great stimulus and creativity, and it added to the balance and depth of the report.

The report itself has edged its way quietly into the bookshelves and thinking of much of the educational leadership of the country. One can regret that the report did not arrive with more dazzle, or immediately spring into legislative being, but the chemistry of the country apparently has not been appropriate.

In the meantime the tragedies of urban education—the faceless millions of children lost to the poverty cycle or worse —are abscessing. There is a kind of kinetic energy building, one that can be channeled toward tremendous growth and one that is dangerously susceptible to sparks. This country has harnessed explosive energy for human dignity and progress before, and it now has that chance in its very own urban backyard.

4

The Politics of Urban Education

by Anita F. Allen

Mrs. Allen was president of the District of Columbia Board of Education from January, 1970, to November, 1971. She was first appointed to the Board in 1967, and she was elected at-large in 1968 to the first elected Board of Education in the city. She served as vice-president of the Board from July 1967 until her election to the presidency. She earned a reputation of deep concern for improving the quality of education in the classroom and is known as an "in-fighter" within the system.

A native of Washington, D.C., and product of the District of Columbia public school system, she matriculated at Howard University (B.A.) and the University of Chicago (M.A.). She also studied on the graduate level in the School of Government and Public Administration at American University in Washington.

She is a career administrator in the Federal Government with twenty years of experience in several federal agencies. For several years she taught at Howard University.

I view urban education from the perspective of one who has served on the board of education of one of our great and profoundly troubled cities, two years as vice president and two years as president. I am particularly concerned here with the politics of urban education.

When one speaks of our troubled cities, one thinks almost automatically of poor and inadequate housing; of social services too limited to meet the overwhelming needs. One thinks of the unemployed, the underemployed, the uncared-for ill, the lonely aged, the restless and bitter youth. But, above all, one thinks of the overcrowded, unresponsive, frequently dreary public schools, faithfully graduating thousands of young men and women unprepared either for higher education or for jobs. The public school systems in our large urban areas have failed to provide even minimal education, and there is little reason to believe that improvements generated from within the system will come soon enough or be significant enough to reverse the present cycle of retardation. Nonetheless, if public education is to survive as an institution, fundamental reforms are necessary. Those of us who believe that reforms must come from within the system have an obligation to make those necessary reforms "happen."

I attended public schools in the District of Columbia during the pre-1954 era of legal school segregation. The schools were "separate" and not "equal," but many of them and certainly the best of them were far superior to most public schools currently in operation in the District. What has happened to the quality of public education over the past eighteen years? One wonders whether it is the caliber or dedication of teachers that has changed or whether the students have changed or whether the society itself has so changed as to bring us to where we are today. Almost instinctively one would say that all three components in the educational process have changed—teachers and other school personnel, children and their parents, and the world around us.

This issue is intimately tied to another one: Whom do we hold responsible for the small degree of learning taking place—the school personnel, the children, or the society? Once more we might say that all three must bear a part of the responsibility—the school personnel because they have indicated willingness and qualifications to teach by accepting their positions; the children because much depends on their receptivity, determination, and ability; and the society because it has the power to insist—if it so desires—that quality education be provided for all children.

Personally, I tend to hold the paid professionals and the lay board of education primarily responsible for the caliber of our public schools, because society and parents and students have placed their confidence in them. It is the professionals who in the first instance must try to accomplish what needs to be accomplished to improve public education.

It is true that students and parents are burdened with problems not of the school's making and that these problems have an impact on the way in which a child learns in school. But experience shows that if the teacher or principal or administrator is concerned enough about educating children, some seemingly insoluble problems can be dealt with successfully. At the same time it is the responsibility of the board of education—on behalf of all citizens—to insist that the professionals, from the superintendent to the classroom teacher, fulfill their obligation to educate the children.

A civilized society clearly has a responsibility to *all* its members. Thus, educationally and economically disadvantaged persons who must cope with a multitude of problems not directly related to the schools need to be assured that there exists somewhere within the society more than just "paper" programs to deal with these problems which can be so devastatingly crippling to the educational process.

No one will dispute the fact that there are historic, economic, and social reasons that can be cited to explain the decline in the quality of public schools. But no amount of explanation can relieve the schools of their absolute responsibility to find a way to educate children, whatever their "problems" may be. It only means that schools must accept the additional task of alerting other public agencies or private resources to their responsibility for the children who are the victims of society's problems. The schools, in short, have a new role to play in the 1970's: They must become the advocates for children vis-à-vis the society as a whole. This means that the failures of public education cannot be excused by pointing to the shortcomings of the world around us. On the contrary, schools must now be judged on the basis of their effectiveness in performing the traditional task—that of freeing the mind—while at the same time acting as public spokesmen for children and their parents.

In my city, Washington, D.C., urban education means 95 percent black education. Whites and, increasingly, the black middle class have moved out of the city to the suburbs; the greater part of the city has taken on all the customary characteristics of an inner city. A black mayor-commissioner and a predominantly black city council were appointed, and shortly afterward, a majority black board of education was appointed (1967). With the passage of the Elected School Board bill, the appointed board was succeeded by an overwhelmingly black school board. With a majority black staff of teachers, principals, and school officers and a predominantly black school population, many believed that the opportunity had arrived for blacks to do for their own what whites had not done—provide sympathetic, meaningful educational experiences so that children would be encouraged to stay in school; welcome parents as participants and observers in the education process; and guarantee improved pupil performance.

Nothing so idealistic, of course, happened. It immediately became clear in Washington as across the country that the distrust of uneducated blacks for better educated blacks— even those who came out of similar backgrounds of poverty

-would be difficult to combat. The natural suspiciousness of low-income blacks was encouraged and "fed" by self-ppointed community leaders. The majority black board of ducation ironically found itself confronted and ridiculed by other blacks. When a program to help the most educationally deprived pupils was instituted, some parents imitated those who claimed to be their spokesmen in doubting their children's capacity. In effect, some said, "Our children cannot earn." The distrust by blacks of blacks is one of the facts of ife that we learn to live with, deal with, and hopefully overcome. Racists have succeeded in causing us to suspect each other.

Without a doubt one of the bitterest experiences that a black leader has to face is rejection by the very blacks whom he is trying to help. And even this could be dealt with if it did not so frequently emerge that the rejection was being initiated and directed by "outsiders"—whites, sometimes the radical-liberals, those with no children in the public schools. One wonders why these so frequently espouse the destruction of persons trying to bring about orderly change—change I like to think of as the revolution from within.

It is my assumption that in Washington, in Detroit, in Philadelphia the forces of reaction are so great, the pull against real change in the schools so strong, the financing of both black and white "fronts" so powerful that poverty-level parents, even middle-class parents, have great difficulty identifying their "friends"—individuals who are trying to improve public education. What seems to happen is that the desire for personal gain, political advantage, and a variety of converging self-seeking interests can and will frustrate any movement toward meaningful change. Those who would try to force schools to respond to the real needs of urban—which is to say poor, black, and brown—children are very likely to be expelled by the system.

Sadly the cry is sometimes for peace and an end to con-

fusion. People too frequently prefer peace at any cost, not
recognizing that those whose present security is tied in with
maintenance of the *status quo* will not give up that *status quo,*
will not redirect resources and energies for the benefit of
the underprivileged without loud cries of anguish. Sometimes
the loudest cries are the death groans of a decadent system.

I believe very strongly that peace at any cost is too big
a price to pay in public education, for it is peace at the cost
of making no basic changes in the system. Very few persons,
however, are willing to figure out what is at stake, determine
who stands for what, and support those whose goals are for
giving children their right to an education. All the forces
of conservatism and radicalism miraculously join hands to
shut off change—the conservative because he is satisfied with
cheating the poor and black and the radical because he prefers to destroy the "system" than to change it.

One also must cope with a conflict of philosophies and
goals of blacks for public education. Black leaders find themselves, for example, torn between the demands of black
separatists and black integrationists. Some argue vigorously
that because integration has not occurred decades after the
law of the land confirmed it, blacks, therefore, should now
go it alone, standing firm against any partial integration,
that they should select only those teachers who understand
black culture, and that at the college level they should rig-
orously segregate blacks in academic programs as well as in
dormitories. Some of these leaders propose integration for
the future when equality has been achieved—integration between equals—some reject it even for the future.

Those who support integration argue that segregated classrooms are innately inferior. They argue that money follows
the white child, and that only integrated classrooms, therefore, will benefit the black child. Whatever course a board
of education charts between integration and separatism must

displease some segment of its constituency. The political problem is acute.

In the larger cities of this nation the racial composition of the population has already gone beyond the point of return. While a majority of persons in this country no longer openly fight school integration, housing segregation, which is still approved and is the way of life, has made the question of school integration almost moot.

The question of metropolitan or statewide districting for racial or economic integration must be dealt with by state legislators or the courts. On the local urban level, one can choose between narrow options: (1) developing a politically "black" school structure in an already racially black system; or (2) developing a high quality education system that will permit its graduates to compete with young people from any other education system, while seizing any opportunities for racially integrated experiences. This latter is my choice and is based on the assumption of educability of the poor and the black and on the necessity to be realistic in recognizing that there is a white majority but that the education of those in urban schools today cannot wait for racial composition of urban schools to change.

The arguments for and against integration are closely tied in with the other no-win debate between those who argue for centralization of authority and those who demand community control. Some say that only with local or community responsibility and complete authority can the schools improve. On the other hand, some who previously supported community, which is to say, black, control now see community control, in practice, as a farce, arguing that power stays with the decision maker downtown and is not transferred to the local group, even when responsibility has been transferred. The argument of nonresponsiveness in the District of Columbia was necessarily weakened as the D.C. board became blacker, but small groups in the community—including the white community—from time to time have urged community control of the schools.

Both the demands for separatism and for community control seem to me to reflect a longing in the black community for quality education. Polls still show that 95 percent of the black community consider education to be the way out of the ghetto for their children. Black parents have seen their children drop out of school or complete upper grades unable to read, write, or communicate, and these parents have reasoned that if they could fire and hire teachers and principals themselves, they could guarantee that dedicated, effective teachers would teach their children. They refuse to subject their children to rejection by the white community; separatism, therefore, would seem to be the answer.

All such answers have been dominated by a feeling of powerlessness to compel schools to do what parents have been unable to do for their children. One sign of this feeling of powerlessness in the black community has been apathy toward almost every effort to involve the community in school affairs. The city-wide elections for ward and at-large members of the board of education have drawn fewer and fewer concerned citizens, especially among those with the most to gain from a responsive board. Even elections for community school boards in the three areas of the District of Columbia where such elections are held drew disappointingly small numbers of voters. Further, too few of those elected then served faithfully or regularly.

Dr. Marilyn Gittell, professor of political science, Queens College, New York, in testifying before Senator Mondale's Select Committee on Equal Education Opportunity, reported a somewhat different reaction in New York Ctiy. She is quoted as saying: "More than 25 percent of the normally apathetic community people vote in these [demonstration school] elections compared to the average 10 percent voting in the [city-wide] decentralization election of 1970." She stated that this "indicates that there is some difference in response according to how people perceive what it is they are engaged in."

Often, it seems, the arguments for separatism and for local control are raised by those with little or no interest in public education itself but with much personal power to gain in taking over control of the most visible social agency in the community. Such individuals hope to build from community control of the schools to control of the community as a whole; for them, control of the schools is only a stepping stone. Such "leadership" is often cruelly indifferent to the educational needs of the children.

For a board, the political dilemma is serious—those who struggle most aggressively for power are often those who are least committed to children.

As a matter of fact it is always difficult to determine who the "community" is and to be sure that one is involving the real "community" and not someone who happens on the right spot at the right time. The District of Columbia board of education found in its "community" meetings that the same people traveled from one end of the city to the other, not for the purpose of improving schools but rather to get the visibility and exposure provided by the news media.

I especially resented having these "school opportunists" drag some children out of the schools to demonstrate for the slightest reason. Frequently the subject of the demonstration was foreign to public education and more appropriate as a cause for demonstration by the fathers or mothers of the school children than by the young people themselves. The political use of school children by a few confronts board members and top administrators of the school system with difficult decisions, since these persons may be sympathetic to the cause but opposed to having the children in their charge manipulated for political purposes.

Beyond the conflicting elements of the black community, a board of education in a predominantly black system must understand the role of the minority white constituency, as well.

The white minority with children in the public schools is a powerful bloc indeed. This group demands higher quality education as a price for remaining in the public school system; they wish to maintain the level of quality which predominantly white schools have maintained over the years, while in the rest of the city achievement levels have steadily declined. The difficult decision for the board member is how to protect quality education in one area while equalizing expenditures of appropriated funds and attaining quality for *all* schools in the city. Inevitably, with decreasing amounts of money available, equalization means reducing allotments for those areas which are better off. Yet, with decrease in school expenditures in white areas will come an accelerated exodus from the public schools. The impact of the white community on public education is apparent when one realizes that as whites leave the public schools, the percentage of funds for the public school system in the total city budget declines. As the white community loses interest in public education, the white community's priorities shift; for example, increased expenditures for the District of Columbia police force were supported while the school budget dropped from 25 percent to 20 percent of the total city budget.

Many blacks, like myself, know that large sums must be appropriated for mandatory increases; whites with congressional or city-hall contacts could obtain those increases and sufficient other resources if their priorities included the education of our children. Yet public education is no longer high priority for whites because so few white children remain in the public schools. Politically this is a vicious cycle.

Black educational leadership must also face the fact that the white middle and upper class shares with many blacks a distrust of the educated, moderate black. Liberal whites, even conservative whites, may support, even encourage, the insulting, uninformed, rhetoric-dispensing black. The reason is apparent: Many do not respect in blacks the qualities they respect in themselves. They expect blacks to be blatant. Although such whites see themselves as cultivated and moderate, the black who labors to bring about meaningful change for the black child in the classroom and who does so by adopting reasonable means is threatening to them. Whites do not understand and cannot control the moderate, educated black, and therefore, they seek to undo him. Ironically, the noisy, ostensibly militant black is easier to exploit and use. Whites *must* control, even when they are a minority. They seek blacks who will permit this.

Of sometimes greater significance is the white control of the press and other opinion-making public media. A black cannot help having a sense of frustration when an editorial or a news story is slanted, because he realizes that the white man, even in a nearly black city, still holds the key to what the public knows or does not know. The political implications for education are obvious.

The conflict over integration exists in the white community, as in the black, but the grounds are different. On this question of integration, some whites believe that their children and all children suffer from the existence of racial isolation and recognize that they are fighting a losing battle as their friends move out of the city or transfer their youngsters into private schools. But a number of whites who support integration support only a one-way movement of children—from the black community to the white—and encourage this movement not as a means to quality education for blacks but as a way to utilize more fully white schools that are otherwise under capacity—and thus to keep them open.

However, a significant group of whites feel that separatism

and local control are the answer for the white minority. They may push for a city-wide network of community-controlled school systems; but the net effect of such a strategy would be to permit the generally more affluent, better educated, frequently more concerned white, or white and upper class blacks, to "secede," in effect from the public school system.

Those who support this approach seem, in my view, to be desperately seeking to stem the tide of deteriorating public schools and declining quality of public education for their children. One cannot argue with this aim. But the means selected may lead to the opposite of the goal they seek.

An urban board of education dealing with the necessary politics of education also must find a way of handling educational faddism. Defining quality education is difficult enough, but there can be tremendous differences of opinion about how to achieve it. Upper-class whites, their black neighbors and black, predominantly lower- and middle-income, groups do not agree on the means to adopt. Few blacks to whom I have talked are concerned with extensive reliance on audiovisual techniques; few blacks are interested in open classrooms. Whites are greatly concerned with both. Blacks, for their part, give high priority to the mastery of basic academic skills. Nothing else will contribute so much to the child's self-concept and happiness. Whites on the other hand, knowing their children have been given that mastery, feel freer to turn their attention to broader questions of creativity, exploration, self-determination, and independence. Blacks are fighting for an education that will permit them to survive, that will give them reasonable life-style options. This difference in priorities leads to additional problems for a black board of education.

A black board member cannot afford to have the most skillful teachers drained from the inner city to "open up" classrooms in white neighborhoods unless such educational innovations and experiments can be instituted without undue financial advantage over the black community. The most skillful teachers belong where the need is greatest.

But perhaps the most important and most difficult of all political problems faced by a board of education is the educational bureaucracy itself. Here, I must necessarily speak in broad terms, with apologies to the many dedicated, highly qualified teachers, school officers, and employees scattered throughout our public school systems. The fact is that it is the absolute resistance of the bureaucracy that is the primary obstacle to change. If the board of education requires change in the way in which the bureaucracy views its obligation to teach children; if it requires change in work hours or in the work year, or change in the way people relate to each other, or in the testing schedule, or in methods of evaluation, unity of opposition among the disparate paid professionals in the school system from beginning teacher to superintendent is the inevitable response. The educational bureaucracy is truly self perpetuating, omniscient, omnipotent. It counts on being able to outlast any superintendent and any board member, and it generally can.

The bureaucracy, supported by the hoary teacher-college structure, maintains that job security is its due and that it alone must be responsible for evaluation of performance. Pupil achievement and what happens to the child in the classroom is not the priority.

Militant unionism among professionals seems concerned primarily with working conditions; a requirement that the academic achievement of children be regarded as relevant to a teacher's employment is never even considered. The principle of accountability for performance has not been accepted. Plans for reorganization or for staff development all stop short of requiring teachers to teach or administrators to administer.

Probably the majority of the paid professionals in our school system do not even believe that the children in their classrooms can learn; therefore, they do not try to teach them. Many do not know how to teach; they show up every day, keep the class the required length of time, and turn in necessary reports at the end of the school year. But they do not teach. A number of children have asked my help in getting teachers to teach them. They do not want teachers to be big sisters or big brothers full of small talk about personal activities—they simply want to be taught.

Boards of education receive from the professional staff numerous excuses for failure to teach. Yet board members, parents, and taxpayers cannot justify this failure, especially at an increased annual cost. Even middle-class children are failing, though they go to school regularly, are highly motivated, are well fed and clothed, and are reasonably healthy. How can this failure be explained away? Something, we submit, must be wrong with the system, not with the child.

An important part in the puzzle called urban education is held by students; they will not be silenced, they recognize that they have rights—and the most basic of these rights is the right to an education. But students, still generally disorganized, indicate their dissatisfaction in contradictory ways: They drop out of school as soon as the law allows, or sooner, or they form small but vocal groups demanding changes in the curriculum or in services or materials provided. Though these demands generally are received by a sympathetic board, these piecemeal reforms are not enough. Major surgery in the system is required. Major surgery will cause pain to the bureaucracy, but without it the system will not survive.

The potential influence and power of parent groups have not yet been recognized by parents themselves. Parents generally do not realize that the educational bureaucrats work for *them*. Parents have been rebuffed so often that they fail to insist through sustained efforts in their PTA's or their home and school associations on accountability by the professionals.

I have not forgotten a conversation I had with a principal of a troubled junior high school in a troubled black community after I joined the board of education. When an immediate solution to a pressing problem had been agreed to, I asked if he thought the longer range, more encompassing solution might not be for him to work more closely with community leaders and parent groups. His candid, but shocking, response was that he did not see this as his role! I doubt that he or any other principal in most city school systems would make the comment today, but many teachers and principals and other school officials *feel* that way.

Local politicians, civil rights leaders, or other public figures give little support to a board of education. In my experience, a local leader often looks for the popular position, jumps on the platform, and leads the march. Nor does an abrupt about-face bother him. A classic example occurred in a board meeting called to discuss closing the schools to commemorate the deaths of Martin Luther King and Malcolm X. A board member stated loudly, "We can't close down the schools every time one of these boys gets knocked off!" Only a few days later the same board member presented "my black brothers from the Malcolm X Committee" and asked for favorable consideration of their request to close the schools.

I can understand almost every position and point of view but not this type of opportunism.

Finally, a board of education faced with the responsibility of educating children must confront the wavering, indefinite, often negative influences of local, state, and federal governmental structures. In the District of Columbia, as may be true elsewhere, the educational budget is determined not by need but by arbitrary limitations unrelated to programs or plans.

The indefiniteness of appropriations, delay, and consequent insufficient planning become a part of the way of life in urban school systems. Political considerations deter-

mining what money is available limit administrative flexibility. Even court decisions sometimes add to the problem.
The recent decision by Judge Skelly J. Wright in the *Hobson
v. Hanson* case, requiring equalization of expenditures for
salaries in elementary schools unless justifiable on the grounds
of compensatory education or the like, presented a monumental problem for the District of Columbia school district.
The board, debating whether to appeal, voted instead to
equalize. Yet it recognized that if older teachers, who because
of longevity receive higher salaries, are moved to inner city
schools, better educational opportunity for inner city black
children will not be a necessary result. Having previously
equalized material resources and now teacher salaries within
a narrow range, we still face in every large city school district
the difficult task of obtaining equalization in educational
yield.

Where, we may ask ourselves, does that leave a troubled
board of education in a troubled city and what are the pros-
pects for the future of black education?

There are some hopeful signs on the horizon. The total
community is slowly becoming aware that improved performance of students is mandatory and that new ways of
conducting educational business must come first. When one
talks with individual teachers, school administrators, parents,
citizen groups, one recognizes that they have in common a
basic longing to make things happen for the children. They
may show distrust, defensiveness, wariness, but still they are
aware that the day of reckoning and accountability is at hand.

Despite all the problems and dilemmas, I sense a basis for
optimism, at least on the District of Columbia educational
scene. The fact that the board of education was willing to
stand together on a belief in the educability of the normal
child and to hold paid professionals responsible for children's
achievement is a major step forward. The shock waves have
not yet stopped reverberating, but the board held to this

position long enough so that at least every major school officer knows he cannot be publicly against accountability for achievement.

The board, in adopting the Academic Achievement Plan developed by Dr. Kenneth B. Clark and the Metropolitan Applied Research Center, disdained the customary socio-economic excuses for failing to teach the poor and the black child. It called for an end to the useless wringing of hands and called for forthright movement by the administration to concentrate school resources so as to end academic retardation. The plan at this writing has not actually been implemented, but community determination that this plan be tried is still alive.

The District of Columbia board is also moving to develop methods to recognize superior teacher ability to meet student needs and to assist his peers. Like most big city school boards, the District of Columbia board feels that it must begin moving in the direction of rewarding professional educators on the basis of ability to meet student needs.

Other hopeful signs of meaningful educational improvement have appeared in public school systems in Oakland, California, in Gary, Indiana, and in Kansas City and St. Louis, Missouri.

The concerned public must insist that teachers, principals, and other school officers unite with parents, students, and taxpayers on the issue of teaching children. Political jockeying for leadership or control must be put aside while responsible citizens join together to save a generation of children in urban centers unable to save themselves without help. There is no other question more urgent, no other call so clear.

With love, hopefully, we can yet find a unifying goal that will preempt all other less noble, more self-serving goals. Educate our children we must, for the future of the nation depends on it.

5

Issues in Urban Education

A speech delivered to the student body at State University College at New Paltz, New York, in November, 1971

by Kenneth B. Clark

Dr. Clark is a distinguished professor of psychology at the City College of the City University of New York and president of the Metropolitan Applied Research Center, Inc. He has also been a member of the New York State Board of Regents since 1965 and is a member of the Board of Trustees of the University of Chicago. A president of the American Psychological Association and former president of the Society for the Psychological Study of Social Issues, he has taught at Queens College and, since 1942, at the City College of the City University of New York. He has been visiting professor at Columbia University, the University of California at Berkeley, and Harvard University. Dr. Clark has served as social science consultant to the NAACP, as adviser to the State Department, and as consultant to a number of foundations, private corporations, and educational institutions. He was awarded the Spingarn Medal from the NAACP in 1961 and the Kurt Lewin Memorial Award from the Society for Psychological Study of Social Issues in 1966. He has been granted honorary degrees by numerous American colleges and universities.

Dr. Clark is the author of several books and articles, including Prejudice and Your Child *(1955); and the prize-winning* Dark Ghetto: Dilemmas of Social Power *(1965);*

74

co-author with Jeannette Hopkins of A Relevant War Against Poverty *(1968); and co-editor with Talcott Parsons of* The Negro American *(1966). His work on the effect of segregation on children was cited by the U. S. Supreme Court in its historic 1954 decision on school desegregation* Brown v. Board of Education.

I believe the issue of education in our urban public school systems to be one of the most important issues confronting this nation at this time. I sometimes qualify this statement by saying "one of the most important *domestic* issues," leaving room for those of us who believe that the idiocy of the Vietnam situation is critical and for those who want to rank things in order of importance or hierarchy. We probably *should* leave room for overseas or international issues and rank them in terms of their importance and separate them from domestic issues. I sometimes make this concession in ordering and separating the importance of domestic issues from the importance of international affairs.

I'm not sure I want to do this anymore. I am coming closer to the opinion that the quality of education provided for the human being in our big city public schools may be the number one issue facing the United States today, in that it is an issue which will determine whether the flamboyant, the ambivalent, paranoid unrealities which I think are inherent in the adventure in Southeast Asia will or will not continue after this war is terminated.

I won't persist in any discussion of the interrelatedness of the chronic inefficiency of American public education on the elementary and secondary level and the continuation of international racially tainted policies and adventures. I will only summarize with the statement that I am obsessed with the notion that until we do something to raise significantly the efficiency and the effectiveness of public education in the United States, we will always be on the brink of disaster in terms of the solution of other domestic problems and also in terms of our posture in international affairs.

The problem of the public schools, the nature of the crisis, is embarrassingly obvious. Study after study has shown that those schools attended by predominantly black, Puerto Rican, Mexican-American, and low-income white students are criminally inefficient in providing these students with the type, quality, and effectiveness of education that will make them able to compete with more privileged youngsters at any public, parochial, or private school in this country. It is now common knowledge that, on the average, underprivileged, minority-group youngsters attending schools that are homogeneous in terms of their underprivileged status are at least two or three and often four or five years retarded in the basic academic skills which seem essential for a constructive role in the society or further academic work. We've known this in New York City for at least the last two decades, and the outcry in New York City in the 1950's led to examination of these data and to comparable data in other cities of this nation. There is not a single exception anywhere in this country to the basic finding that racially homogeneous, predominantly black or minority-group schools are inefficient in terms of providing these children with an effective education and that the norm is underachievement in these schools.

In New York State, for the last four years, there has been a pupil-evaluation program in regard to Title III, whereby the State Education Department receives information on academic achievement in the basic skills of reading and arithmetic for all schools in the State. By means of this program, it is possible to compare the efficiency of various schools on the basis of the achievement of their children. Accordingly, the State Education Department and the educators in New York City have known for the past four years that on the basis of the results of this pupil-evaluation, pupil achievement testing program of the State Education Department, the children attending the New York City public schools are the most short-changed children educationally in this state; that the New York City public schools have the highest proportion of children who are below the minimal achievement level at the various grades tested in reading and arithmetic. There are also some schools in New York City, obviously predominantly black and Puerto Rican, in which the percentage of children below a minimal acceptability of achievement which is significantly below norm, is as high as 70 or 80 percent, and consistently so. I repeat, we have known this in the State Education Department for about four years or more. The Board of Education in the city of New York has known that the majority of its schools in the public school system are turning out functional illiterates, young people who are clearly incapable of competing with other more privileged youngsters from more advantaged communities and homes, and not a single thing has been done about it.

Within recent years, actually within the last two decades, black people, the victims of this kind of criminal insensitivity and inefficiency on the part of the educational system, have attempted to do something to increase the chances of their children's being given the kind of education which will make for a more constructive life. The victims have had to take this burden on because the more privileged members of our society have been able for the most part to avoid the horrors of seeing their children undereducated and dehumanized in the public schools, either by escaping to private or parochial schools, or, if they stay in the public school system, by developing private preserve schools within the public school system. In New York City, for example, there are a number of schools which are in fact private public schools and which are defended as such. The Bronx High School of Science, for example, is an illustration of what I mean by a private public school, that is, one that is available to privileged, more advantaged groups in society in addition to private and parochial institutions. The classic escape tactics of middle-class urban whites, by the way, also seem to be true of middle-class blacks who, understandably, seek to flee from the dehumanizing public school system by removing their children and sending them to private schools.

As a result, the rest of the public schools regress in aggression law fashion to increased inefficiency, and, until rather recently, families who remained were required to accept the stagnation, the pathology, the horror of, I repeat, *criminally* inefficient pubic schools—public schools that are not only inefficient but seek to justify their inefficiency by blaming the victims of their inefficiency; by saying that these children are not being educated because they're uneducable . . . or because they're discipline problems . . . or because their families are not interested in education.

The educational establishment in charge of our public schools in large urban cities has built up a codification of explanations for the inefficiency which projects the cause upon the victims of the inefficiency and insists that the schools and those who are responsible for the schools are not to blame. They've been reinforced by the prestige of psychologists, educators, and most recently by the vice-president of the Educational Testing Service, Henry Dwyer, who has engaged in a sham of accountability design with the Board of Education of the city of New York and when one looks at the details of his accountability design, one finds that it is the codification of the alibis for the continuation of the inefficiency in the education of minority group youngsters.

This is the situation: The public schools, at least in regard to the education of minority groups and lower status group youngsters, have now become the chief instruments in the blockage of mobility for presently powerless lower status groups. This history and tradition of American public schools as the instrument for facilitating mobility, as the chief vehicle through which waves of immigrant groups of eastern, southern, or any other part of Europe could, in fact, come to America and use free public education as the most effective instrument for upward economic and social mobility, are now no longer a fact for dark-skinned minority groups. And, the public schools have assumed and are using quite effectively their power to make the powerless status of these groups permanent; to maintain stratifications and distinctions between dark-skinned minorities and upwardly mobile white groups, so that it is no longer necessary for prejudiced business and industry personnel managers to effect job discrimination. The discrimination is accomplished for them at the source; the public schools have now become the chief and most effective instrument of economic discrimination and academic discrimination at the higher educational levels.

I am fully aware of the fact that this is a harsh indictment. I've been criticized frequently for my ability to overstate, overdramatize the issue. I can only say to you what I've said to critics in the past. I do not believe that I am overstating or overdramatizing. If anything, I believe that I am understating the reality and that, were it not for the fact that the victims of this educational monstrosity that has become our urban public school systems are black or dark-skinned, the reality would be the basis for a national crisis, a political crisis of the first magnitude.

The only reason that this reality can be ignored or that those who insist upon calling the public's attention to it can be accused of exaggeration is that the public schools are damaging those human beings which this society considers expendable. In other words, this society has opted to permit public education to destroy the capacity of those human beings whom it is unwilling to accept, to prevent them from becoming effective or constructive members of a larger society. I say that because I think the facts clearly support it.

If one looks at the history of attempts at remedying this obvious educational disaster which characterizes public education for minority group youngsters from urban systems, one finds a history of failure. For example, the initial attempt to remedy this disaster was through desegregation; but desegregation has been aborted by tokenism for the most part. In New York City, the attempts at desegregation led to the busing of black children from predominantly black schools to allegedly integrated schools; but this tactic merely led to the intensification of segregation *within* these allegedly integrated schools. We're in New York City now. I'm not talking about Jackson, Mississippi, I'm not talking about Birmingham, Alabama, I'm talking about our own city, New York. Black children were bused to so-called integrated schools and kept in isolation, kept in separate classes, taken to the cafeteria when other more precious children would not be contaminated by the color of their skin. And, there was really no great loss when this inhuman form of desegregation was abandoned. The black communities did not rise up in indignation when this kind of cruelty perpetrated on our children was terminated. We have as high a degree of racial isolation and homogeneity in the New York City public school system today, if not higher, than we had in 1954–1955 when the issue was first raised. And, I repeat, there was no weeping at the termination of busing because it was clear that those who controlled the system, the Central Board of Education, the administrators, were willing and able to inflict this kind of cruelty on other human beings, not only with impunity but with the sanction of educational jargon.

So, the attempts at desegregation by the administrators in order to increase academic achievement of children in New York City was abandoned by all, and, interestingly enough, was followed by another method on the part of the victims, the method and the technique of decentralization. Let me remind you that the first major demand for decentralization in the IS-201 Complex situation had a history which very few people recall or would like to recall. The initial demand of the IS-201 parents and community was not for decentralization, the initial demand of those parents was for desegregation. The Board of Education and the Superintendent of Schools met the demand of the parents for desegregation of the IS-201 Complex by saying that it was impossible because white parents would not permit their precious children to be bused into Harlem. It was all right for black children to be exposed to whatever horror resided in Harlem—that was all right for black children—but white children could not be exposed to it. This is the kind of society in which we live—a society that says that some human beings should be conserved and protected by the educational system but other human beings are expendable. I personally heard this said by responsible, decent officials at 110 Livingston Street [headquarters of the New York City Board of Education]. When the parents of IS-201 were told the same thing, they replied, "To hell with you. To hell with your desegregation . . . Give us these schools. We will take desegregated schools and we will run them our way. Obviously, you don't give a damn about our children. But, we do. We will protect them."

I want to remind you that the decentralization issue came directly out of the persistent and chronic frustration on the part of black parents to get effective desegregation in New York City. The black parents and we educators who were truly concerned found a viable common meeting ground on the basis of this frustration. We first became totally identified and functioned as allies in trying to get some kind of honest decentralization in the New York City public school system. Our rationale was that if this society was so inflicted and inhibited by racism, then let us take this racism and see if we can work with it. Let us get the Central Board to give power to the people in the local communities, so that they will have the power to exact accountability from teachers, administrators, advisers. In those days we really believed that this would be an answer to the question of achievement.

We believed this because we saw desegregation was not an answer, because that was aborted.

Our naïveté was soon indicated by the discovery that the assistance to desegregation on the part of the Central Board was merely a prelude to their massive resistance to any effective decentralization. It became very clear that the Central Board and its bureaucracy were not willing to provide the local people with even the opportunity to fail.

I threw myself into the decentralization struggle, not because I was sure that it would succeed in significantly raising the academic achievement of predominantly minority-group youngsters. I threw myself into this struggle because I knew that it couldn't be more of a failure than the centralized operation. I knew there was nothing that local school boards, controlled by the people in the local community, could do that could be more damaging to the children in the elementary schools than that which the Central Board and the Central administrators were doing or failing to do.

The summary observation here is that decentralization, like desegregation, met such massive resistance that we don't have any evidence. We really don't know; we won't know, because as of today the decentralization act is actually mere smoke screen, hiding the fact that there is no actual decentralization. The local school boards *do not* have the actual power to determine the quality of education presented to their children. They *do not* have the power to recruit, evaluate, or dismiss teachers on the basis of performance.

The power in the New York City public school system over the quality of education for minority-group children is in the hands of the UFT (United Federation of Teachers), the Supervisors Association, and their representatives in the higher echelons of administration. And it is clear to me that there is no evidence that these sources of power are any more concerned with the conservation of minority-group youngsters, any more concerned with providing them with effective education now than they were five, ten, or twenty years ago.

Another technique which has been used to cure the blight of urban education for minority children is compensatory education, pumping money into programs designed to enrich or compensate for the inefficiency in the basic education of these children. Compensatory education has been profitable; no one has resisted, to any great degree, this approach to remedying the massive inferiority of the education provided for minority-group students. I suspect that one of the reasons compensatory education met massive resistance is that it is minimal in effect. No matter how you look at it, it is still a very small fraction of children who are being destroyed by the inefficiency in the public school system and who are capable of being salvaged by compensatory educational programs on the secondary or the higher educational levels. In fact, Albert Shanker, the head of the UFT, can quite truthfully say that he is a champion of compensatory educational programs. What he cannot say is that he is a champion of programs designed to raise the quality of education in all of the schools in New York City to the level where compensatory educational programs would no longer be necessary. In fact, he is on record against any genuine form of accountability.

But does that mean that we have to give up in a sense of total despair, futility, failure, and defeat? I don't think so. I don't think that we have to give up, and it may very well be that the only reason I don't think we are doomed to total failure is that maybe I'm like an old firehorse; that in a sort of Pavlovian conditional reflex, in a sort of pattern, I respond automatically to some kind of action as long as the problem persists—in spite of continued indications that there are some problems that seem to resist any possible humane, decent solution. And, certainly, they are in our history.

Our history would not support starry-eyed optimism concerning the possibility of our educational bureaucracies, particularly those that control our public school system, being responsive to changes that will benefit minority-group youngsters by way of providing them with effective education. Yet in spite of this negative evidence I still believe that it is possible to change the situation, to achieve a positive resolution to the urban public school crisis. I believe it is possible to the point where I started our staff at MARC on the task of designing an academic achievement program for the city of Washington, D.C. In our enthusiasm to get this program adopted and implemented, we did something we've never done before—we met our deadline! The Board in Washington asked us to have a design in their hands by June 1 of 1970 and by June 5 I was on the shuttle taking it to them, and, I think, on June 6 they passed it.

This design toward the attainment of high academic achievement among minority group youngsters is a very simple design, and I won't presume to give you the details of it. The only thing that I will tell you is that the essence of the design is: If these children are effectively taught, and if a public school system is really seriously interested and concerned with the education of these children, these children, like other human beings, will learn.

The first order of business should be to address the problem of teacher motivation, then the preparation of teachers, and the kind of education and supervision which is given to them. And, looking at the certification process, what we suggested is that teachers have as important a job as physicians, that the destiny and the disciplined intellectual basis of life for a human being are as important as the health of the human being. So, we used the training of physicians as our model for the main suggestion of our design; namely, if you look at medical education, you find that merely because a young man received his M.D. degree does not mean the society sets him free to practice medicine willy-nilly.

The society considers the M.D. merely the beginning of the training process rather than the end of it and requires that physicians have post-degree training as interns and residents. We offered this model to Washington, D.C. We thought it shameful to take a young person out of teacher-training school and just throw him into an urban classroom, where he gets minimal, if any, supervision. Instead, what the teacher-training institute should do, together with the Board of Education in Washington, is to take the young person who comes out with a teacher-training degree in June, and if he is employed in that system, designate him as a "resident teacher" for the first three years of his employment. For these three years it would be the responsibility of the teacher-training institution together with the supervisors of that system to continue to offer help and support and continued education, supervision and training in the classroom. And if, at the end of three years, that teacher demonstrates the ability to be an effective teacher, then certification should be given and that teacher moved to the next level as "staff teacher." The "staff teacher" would have less supervision and, on the basis of demonstrated performance, could move to the third level of "senior teacher."

Again, the evaluation by which such promotions would be made would be in terms of demonstrable effectiveness, in terms of the achievement of the children. The final level would be that of master teacher, and the responsibility of master teacher would be that of helping in the growth and development of the staff teachers, the resident teachers, and so forth.

We believed that the major problem that had to be faced and dealt with in raising the academic achievement of underprivileged youngsters was the problem of the professional perspective and image of the teaching profession. That supervision and accountability were essential and were absent in the present situation. Needless to say, the teachers' organizations and the administration in Washington reacted by rejecting this and other suggestions.

As of now, and I shift for my conclusion to Washington, D.C., the stark truth that I learned by moving from New York to the Washington area was that we cannot explain the resistance of educational bureaucracies to improving the effectiveness and the quality of education for minority-group youngsters in terms of the simplistic explanations of black against white, or white against black. I make now the public confession that as long as we were just working on the resistance in New York City, I believed that the basis of the resistance was that the power in New York City in the educational establishment, in the supervisors' association, in the teachers' union was predominantly, if not exclusively, white. *And,* that the children with whom we were concerned were predominantly nonwhite. Therefore, we had a sensitivity to them, but the power structure had no sensitivity to them. And to me, the racial explanation was obvious, although I did not publicly make that point.

The horrible lesson which the Washington experience has taught me is that, in spite of the fact that the Board of Education there accepted this design for higher academic achievement of children in the Washington school system as early as June, 1970, and we are now coming to the end of this academic year, and not a single thing has been done to improve the quality of education for the children in Washington —and that at the end of this school year they will be as retarded in basic academic subjects as they were at the end of the last school year, if not more so. The horrible lesson which I've learned from these facts is that race is not the definitive explanatory factor because the Board, the Superintendent of Schools in Washington, the head of the teachers union in Washington are black. The teachers who have argued that black children should not be required to learn because if they do, they will merely enter into a white racist society—as if reading were the white exclusive privilege—these have been black teachers.

What I've learned is that the enemy is more formidable than just color; America's brand of racism infects both blacks and whites. It permeates institutions and becomes institutionalized, and many of my black adversaries in Washington did not realize that they had been brainwashed in their willingness to accept the role of blocking any significant program to improve the education for black children. And, what was even more ironic, this blocking was often done under the rhetoric of black militants. I heard some of the same explanations of why this program should not be implemented in Washington coming out of the mouths of blacks that I heard in New York coming out of the mouths of whites.

I promised you that I would not end on a pessimistic note. I always promise my students that every lecture that seems to be going in the direction of the negative will be automatically swung around for a Hollywood ending. They must live happily ever after, even if we have to kill them in order for them to do so.

As long as we're alive, we're going to continue to fight for these children's right to educational equity and equality. We're not going to permit defeats to make us retreat. We will retreat only when we have been really bludgeoned into insensitivity.

Now for my conclusion. I pretended to be reluctant in accepting the invitation to come here only because I wanted desperately to be able to invite the School of Education, the Department of Education in New Paltz, to engage directly and actively with some of us in New York City to continue to try to improve the quality of education, the quality of teacher training, and maybe to really propose marriage, marriage in the innovation of a new approach to teacher training. A marriage that would give New Paltz the opportunity to demonstrate that of all of the units of the State University system, it is the most imaginative and innovative in the training of teachers for our urban, or I'll even say suburban, school systems, to be the first institution to say We are not content to place young people in classrooms where they sink or swim on their own and we are prepared to work with any intelligent, concerned educational system that would dare to carry out this experiment with us.

This would be, I think, an important contribution to a problem of human educational justice. Thank you.

Questions posed by the audience and Dr. Clark's answers

QUESTION: Do you think there's any hope in decentralization?

DR. CLARK: Frankly, I don't think it's going to come in any other than sham form. I think the present decentralization in New York City is not really decentralization. It's a pretense of decentralization, when the actual controlling power still is in the Central authority. Now, I don't know that it would guarantee increased efficiency if it did come. I don't know that the bureaucratic stagnation is not so metastasized as to effect and perpetuate the stagnation of the decentralized system. I feel very strongly about it that it's not likely to come anyway so the latter part of the statement is academic.

QUESTION: Does a school of education presently exist that you would recommend we pattern ourselves after?

DR. CLARK: I would suggest that you don't pattern yourself after any existing school of education, that you become models for them.

QUESTION: Dr. Clark, what are your views on the performance contract?

DR. CLARK: May I plead the Fifth on that? Because I am a member of the Board of Regents and our Commissioner here serves at the—what do they say, pleasure?—he serves at the pleasure of the Regents. I don't think it would make any sense to get into a public controversy with the Commissioner whom I like personally and with whom I generally agree. So now you can make your own judgment, you see.

QUESTION: If everyone is aware of the racism in the public school system, why it is allowed?

DR. CLARK: Well, it is allowed, I believe, because this nation has had a history of considering dark-skinned people less than human.

QUESTION: Are white people that sadistic?

DR. CLARK: I'm not going to try to convince you. I can only tell you that every attempt to bring humanity and sensitivity into public education for dark-skinned minority groups has been resisted, and successfully so, so far. I'm a psychologist, but I don't want to get into the question of motivation or intent or sadism. I just want to be as empirical as possible. The fact is that when the New York City Board of Education announced that it was twenty-five million dollars short in meeting its budget for the current school year, this fact triggered massive, indignant insistence on the part of the legislature and on the part of the State Education Department for investigations. I think there are committees from all over Albany now tripping over each other trying to find out, you know, why this happened.

Money is apparently a very important thing for our society and our state. And one of the legislative committees gave a report within a matter of a week or ten days that there's fiscal chaos rampant in the New York City public school system.

Let me remind you what I started my earlier presentation with: We, the Board of Regents, we, the State Education Department, have known for at least five years the fact that the public schools in New York City are educational disaster areas in terms of these minority-group youngsters. We've had no investigation committees. The legislature has not sent down a task force to find out why otherwise normal children should be retarded consistently in reading and arithmetic and the higher the grade, the more they are retarded. We haven't shown any sense of concern or urgency over the fact that a majority, a substantial majority, of black youngsters and Puerto Rican youngsters who come out of the secondary schools or the high schools, general or academic or vocational, have reading scores no higher than the fifth or sixth grade. We haven't addressed ourselves to the educational chaos which is norm. On the contrary, we have accepted the explanations.

QUESTION: You've been brainwashed . . .

DR. CLARK: Yes, we've been brainwashed, because it's easy to brainwash the American public on anything which alludes to, or suggests, or implies, or is even explicit about the inferiority of dark-skinned people, you see. And this is what the educational bureaucracies have done. Quite gentlemanly, by the way. They're not ranting, raving, flagrant racist bigots. Many of the racist ideas that have sustained differential lower status education for black kids have come under the guise of compassionate understanding for their limitations, you know, "You shouldn't frustrate these poor youngsters because they really can't meet the standards of other people."

This is one of the most disturbing things about it. I think that we would have been more honest, white and black, if the alibis for inflicting this kind of educational barbarity upon blacks came in open, obvious, bigotry form. But, when they come in the form of understanding—You know, they come from poor homes, broken homes, no books in the home —they give a list, a litany of the deprivations. What they say in effect is that the symptoms of racist injustice that prevail in the larger society justify the continuation of the inequities in the educational situation.

We have permitted this to happen because these people are black, and America has had a tradition of believing that black people are less than human and, therefore, should not get the same quality of education that other human beings have. And this might be the Achilles heel of America and this is the basis on which I no longer make a distinction between domestic problems and international problems, because it may very well be that the survival or distinction of America as a social system will come out of this very subtle, internal, cancerous, dry-rottish erosion of the educational system. The people who have least to lose by this, by the way, are the blacks who have been deprived.

QUESTION: Dr. Clark, can the schools alone solve this?

DR. CLARK: No. The schools alone cannot solve the problems of all. But the schools can solve the problem of teaching children to read and to do arithmetic and to speak correctly and to write correctly.

QUESTION: But haven't a number of compensatory education programs, working in cooperation with the schools, been successful?

DR. CLARK: There's no question about this. In fact, these compensatory programs that I told you about are always successful. They can always go to the foundations we admire and get more money from them, because they can always demonstrate that if you teach children, they'll learn. The only time they fail is when you try to translate that demonstration into what goes on in the school. The school always finds some reason why it should go on as a demonstration project, but it shouldn't interfere with the normal operating failure of the school.

My wife is a director of a child-guidance clinic at the boundary of Central and East Harlem, and to my knowledge every summer for the last fifteen or so summers, they have had a remedial reading program for the most neglected children— the children whom the schools have given up on because "they just can't read." Well, I remember I was an associate with her, in part, during the first few years of that project where they brought a number of these youngsters into North-side for a four-week intensive remedial reading program—one hour a day five days a week, I think. The first three or four years when I was around (I'm a sort of constitutional skeptic, you know) I didn't believe that this was going to be particularly successful. The first year's result demonstrated that the average gain for reading among these children who were considered incapable of learning to read—the average gain for the four weeks, five days a week, one-hour-a-day session—was one year and eight months.

Well, I said: Ah, you know, this is not a fact. There's something wrong, some kind of selection and, furthermore, we had a foundation grant and I think she told me to write up the results. And I said, no, we can't do this. We'll have to get more data. We'll have to do it a number of years and we'll have to be sure that we are not selecting for success.

So, each year we tried to control variables to see that we were having normal groups of nonachieving youngsters. The results have been consistent from that time up to the present. In fact, if anything, they've gone up.

Now let me tell you another little footnote on these re-sults. We have had consistently positive results that if these children are taught, they will learn and achieve at the same rate as the other group of normal human beings that were taught. The footnote, the fascinating footnote to this is that at the end of the summer they went back into the public schools from which they came, and when they were retested at the end of that academic year, they didn't gain a single bit over what they had gained the previous summer. So, that's where we started comforting ourselves with the notion . . . well, at least they didn't lose in the schools what they gained in the summer in the schools. The schools weren't able to make them unlearn what they had learned. But, they went into the public schools, after the remedial sessions during the summer, and just stayed on a plateau.

QUESTION: Dr. Clark, does your research indicate that a teacher trying hard could do the same thing?

DR. CLARK: No. That's a variable. We did not have twenty-five students for a particular teacher. I suppose the most we ever had for any particular remedial reading session was three or four. We do have data, though, from other sources that approximate the twenty-five to thirty students we've done here, in St. Louis, in the Bonnicker school district under Sam Shepherd's supervision. He got significant increases, but they did not approach what we, what my wife and her staff, got at Northside. But, in a regular school district, with regular classes in a normal pupil/teacher ratio, Sam Shepherd got, he says, "economically, racially deprived youngsters" functioning at grade level norm.

We, unfortunately, have enough exceptions, enough indications that it is possible in a classroom setting with adequately motivated teachers, with adequate supervision, to get deprived children who are not organically deficient functioning at grade level at least, if they are properly taught.

QUESTION: There have been proposals that highly motivated and successful teachers be given some kind of incentive —or reward—for their work in the form of higher pay, and so forth. Why weren't they put into practice?

DR. CLARK: Because it was threatening to the industrial, labor union perspective of teachers' unions. The teachers' union, the American Federation of Teachers, and the local branches in the United States have taken what I consider a very shortsighted and self-defeating perspective of the profession. They have built into their concept of union policy the notion that teachers must be motivated toward mediocrity, if not inferiority. They have taken as rigid policy the notion that there must be no differential pay and that the only basis for differences in remuneration of teachers would be longevity. If you just live long enough, you will get the increment on the basis of living. Well, hell, I don't know of any other profession that considers that a virtue. The differentiated staffing and remuneration on the basis of demonstrated differences in production, skill, performance, contribution to the field is normal operating practice in every professional field that I know of, except teaching. The main objection to our plan on the part of the teachers' union in Washington was that we were saying that teaching is a profession, and that training and incentives, career ladder incentives, tied to demonstrable performance, must be introduced into this profession if there is going to be any change in the present stagnation that I call the professional aggression law of constant or fixed remuneration, without regard to the demonstrations of effectiveness.

But, they succeeded. And one reason they succeeded is because they got our superintendent, who, it would seem to me, appears to be incompetent and weak and unwilling to run the risk of revolt. And, I don't think we're going to change the present situation in our public schools in our cities without some major revolt to the point of catastrophe. I would think that, rationally, it would be better to have the revolt from within the system than to have the victims decide to have the revolt by bombs or dynamite or other forms of totally irrational violence, and it may have to come to that, if the people within the system don't understand that people are not going to tolerate indefinitely the evidence of the dehumanization and the destruction of their children.

II

Blacks and Higher Education

1

Education for Manhood:
A Black Perspective of Higher Education

by Joseph R. Harris

Joseph R. Harris is Associate Dean of Students, Staten Island Community College of the City University of New York, and Director of the College Discovery Program. This program offers special educational resources to students from New York City poverty areas. Mr. Harris has worked and traveled in Africa, the Caribbean, and the United States. A graduate of La Salle College, he holds a master's degree in political science from Fordham University where he is completing his doctoral work in comparative and urban politics.

Toward a Black Perspective

There are three basic problems facing black educators, scholars, and students concerned about higher education. Our primary need is to develop a black perspective of education—a world view which recognizes a community of interests among all people of African descent. Another important task we face is the need to develop a sense of our own history which will enable us to build effective educational institutions in black communities. Finally, we must create for ourselves a new educational model—a black university. This university must serve the real needs of the people of the black world community—those individuals of African descent who live primarily within the triangular area encompassing

Africa, the Caribbean, and the United States. Our cooperative efforts to undertake these essential steps constitute a
historic challenge and define our purpose in the struggle for
black liberation and manhood.

All black colleges and universities have a purpose beyond
that of teaching and doing research. Functioning within a
community which has been deprived of its full maturation,
black institutions of higher education must help their students, and through them, all black men, regain their manhood.

In order to redefine the role of black universities in modern society, it is important to appreciate the fact that the
modern university, as we know it, is a relatively recent phenomenon. Even in the metropolitan centers of the world most
modern universities emerged during the second half of the
last century. It is during this same historical period—a time
of vast social, political, economic, and technological change—
that most black institutions of higher education were developed. It is important for us to keep in mind that the black
university, however, is still in its infancy.

We must be conscious of the fact that black institutions
of higher education were fashioned out of a historical past
in which their primary purpose—a special purpose—was to
"educate" the slave or subject of a colonial empire. This not
too distant past, I contend, has left little opportunity for the
black university to develop its own sense of larger purpose.
Having had its role defined by more powerful external
forces, the black university has essentially trained black people to take their place in a white world.

Aware now, however, that the first law of resistance is survival, we should appreciate the important work done by so-
called "Negro colleges" in the past. No other institutions of
higher learning have ever faced the herculean task of educating vast numbers of former slaves with severely limited
resources. Through great sacrifice this effort has been carried

into this generation. Today we can speak of a black university of tomorrow because we have inherited this foundation. Thus, as I urge consideration of possible alternative courses of action for black institutions of higher education, I am mindful of Du Bois's sage advice: "It is all well enough for us of another generation to wax wise with advice to those who bore the burden in the heat of the day."

Historical Development of Black Universities

We stress the necessity of viewing higher education from a worldwide perspective for three reasons. First, we recognize from a historical perspective that most people in the black world community have had very similar "colonial" educational experiences. Second, we are more conscious today of the relationship between education and political development. Finally, our awareness of the "politics of education" creates the necessity for a new comparative analysis of the purpose and direction of higher education in black communities, especially in Africa, the Caribbean, and the United States of America.

The creation of black institutions of higher education followed similar patterns. This fact is demonstrated by the following analysis of the development of selected universities in the United States, Africa, and the Caribbean.

In the United States

From the earliest history of education in the United States the socioeconomic pattern of division between the races was reflected. Indeed, as Henry Allen Bullock has observed: "In the beginning there was no thought of educating the Negro . . . the plantation economy was intended as a completely rational institution . . . in which each black was to serve as a tool . . . with Negroes conceived of as tools and investments, the rational model required that the master-class relations be structured almost solely along functional lines."

The education of the slave was a matter of little importance in the American social and economic system. Following the acquisition of skills and trades by some slaves, a kind of permissiveness gradually affected the plantation society's policy; thereafter a few educational opportunities were provided for a select group of slaves.

The first educational institutions were founded, mainly by Protestant religious groups, during the middle of the nineteenth century. Colleges established by the black African Methodist Episcopal Church were a notable exception to this rule. Later, with the creation of the Freedman's Bureau, the federal government entered the field. Thereafter, the federal government played a significant role in defining and developing educational opportunities at all levels. Howard University, perhaps the best known black university in America, was founded in 1867, and reflects this pattern of interplay between religious and governmental forces.

The university grew out of contacts between General Otis Howard, Commissioner of the Freedman's Bureau, and members of the First Congregational Society in 1866. The original idea was to establish an educational institution for newly emancipated slaves. The new institution was to be a theological college, but it was decided that a normal school, secular in character, would be more likely to win Congressional approval. Thus, the "Howard Normal and Theological Institute for the Education of Teachers and Preachers" was proposed. By May, 1867, the school's official name became "The Howard University." It was also decided that the school would be open to members of all races and to members of both sexes. In fact, the first students were white girls, children of two of the founders; but in time the institute for the "education of youth" became a predominantly "Negro" university, which has in more recent years become increasingly committed to black education.

The university's charter is an Act of Congress, passed on

March 2, 1867, and sets forth its mission, powers, and form of governance. The Act also established the first regular departments: normal, collegiate, theological, law, medicine, and agriculture. In 1881, following the general expansion of graduate education in America, Howard developed a College of Dentistry, and, subsequently, other graduate faculties. Today, the university is a hybrid—it is privately controlled but largely federally financed.

Thus Howard University symbolizes, in many respects, the "Negro college." It was developed out of the alliance between religious and federal government control of education for "freed" men. To a large extent its mission, powers, and form of governance were dictated by local circumstances. The university is the only federal university in the United States because it was created by an Act of Congress. The original departments and financing authorized at Howard reflected the original economic perspective of the education of black people.

After emancipation, a new economic and political approach was formulated for the development of educational opportunities for black people. Slaves had been trained to work. The ex-slaves had to be taught economic self-sufficiency and how to be "good citizens" of the Union. Such education was to be "special education provided in separate institutions." This pattern of so-called "separate but equal" educational opportunity remained essentially intact until the Supreme Court decision of 1954, when integration of publicly supported institutions became the law of the land.

It is noteworthy, however, that it was not until the student-initiated black rebellions of the early 1960's that fundamental questions were raised within black institutions of higher education about their modern purpose and direction. Until recently the institutional response to the demands of black youth has been limited. In far too many black colleges and universities the response was limited to "Black Studies" models similar to those in white institutions of higher education. This kind of reaction to the legitimate needs of black students to know more about how to improve their communities is unfortunate, especially since most of the serious research about black people was originally conducted in predominantly black colleges and universities during the early part of this century. It remains to be seen if a modern black university can emerge from a colonial past in the United States.

In Africa

The development of the modern university in West Africa had to await the British government's conception of economic and political necessity. Prior to the *Report of the Royal Commission on Higher Education* and that of its *Special Committee on West Africa* in 1945, only three institutions of higher education existed in British West Africa. The oldest, Fourah Bay College in Sierra Leone (1827), was affiliated with Durham University; Prince of Wales College at Achimota, Ghana, was affiliated with London University; and in Nigeria there was a technical college at Yaba. In all three cases, the "colleges" were not capable of awarding a degree, except through their affiliation with a British university.

The Commission's aim was "to prepare the colonies for self-government," and to develop a leadership elite capable of administering the self-governing territories once they became independent. In order to achieve their aims, the Commission recommended:

1. the development of three centers of higher education in British West Africa. They are: a new college at Ibadan in Nigeria; the development of Achimota College on the Gold Coast, and a re-organization, on a new site, of Fourah Bay College in Sierra Leone . . .
2. that the standards of the various stages of the courses proposed should be those of British universities . . .

3. that the cost—1½ million pounds . . . be borne initially by the Colonial Development and Trust Fund; and the quarter of a million annual recurrent expenditure . . . be borne by the West African governments.

The Commission also filed a minority report which called for the establishment of a university college at Ibadan and territorial colleges in all other dependent territories in West Africa linked to the university college.

The Commission's recommendations were implemented in West Africa in 1948, thereby meeting the educational needs of "developing people," as their needs were perceived by the British government. The modern African university, built on the colonial foundation, could not begin to meet the real educational needs of African people until nationhood had been achieved.

In the Caribbean

Until the turn of the twentieth century, higher education in the West Indies, according to Lloyd Braithwaite, a Trinidadian scholar, was: ". . . education of the upper and middle classes for professions, and the development of institutions of higher education had to await the period when these classes were sufficiently concerned with their own problems to wish to have adjustments made." The reasons for this state of affairs are grounded in the development of higher education in the Caribbean.

The earliest efforts to develop higher education in the West Indies (British) were led by religious leaders. Bishop Berkeley in Bermuda attempted to establish a college that was directed toward the needs of the British colonial establishment in the 1740's, but it failed.

Later, toward the end of the nineteenth century, there was an attempt to establish Queens College in Spanish Town, Jamaica. This college failed in 1875, in large measure because it lost local support.

At the beginning of this century, the most developed institution of higher education in the West Indies was the Imperial College of Tropical Agriculture in St. Augustine, Trinidad. It was the base for the development of a university in the West Indies.

The idea of establishing a University of the West Indies was old in origin, the main features having been spelled out in a report by Patrick Keenan in the 1870's. The idea was given impetus by domestic disturbances in the West Indies in 1937–38 and the events surrounding the World War. The Asquith Commission was established in 1943 to look into the problem of higher education in the West Indies area.

The Commission proposed the following:

1. There should be established a University of the West Indies with the status of a University College, affiliated to the University of London.
2. Initially the curriculum should be ". . . limited to the Faculties of arts, science and medicine . . . The subjects to be taught in the University have been chosen with special reference to the West Indian conditions . . ." [However, it is noted in the Report that effort should be made] "to provide a broad cultural education and the Commission has drawn on the experience of the older universities of Great Britain and many of the subjects of study prescribed are identical with those taught in this country."
3. The Commission estimated the costs for the establishment of the University to be 1,630,000 pounds. The method of financing the cost was very similar to the formula suggested for the West African higher education plan.

Thus, Braithwaite points out, the University College of the West Indies, established at Mona, Jamaica, in 1948, was seen by Britain as providing the necessary local leadership within the West Indian area, and it was a projection of the best of traditional British universities abroad. The University was thought to be a "parting gift" of the United Kingdom government. Braithwaite rightly asserts that the whole subsequent history of the University in the area has been an attempt to adapt the British model to the realities of West Indian conditions.

It is worth noting that both in West Africa and in the Caribbean, British colonial educational policy called for: the establishment of university colleges tied to British universities; limiting possibilities for academic input at the local level by placing the traditional emphasis on teaching and research rather than a greater emphasis on extension services and communal development; and the stressing of the fiscal responsibility of the British government, instead of seeking local support in any serious way. There was operative here a rather keen logic, namely, that the universities were a means of binding the colonial areas to the United Kingdom culturally, even though the purported purpose for governmental action was the necessary preparation of colonial people for democratic self-government.

Again, as in Africa, the people of the Caribbean had to await political independence before they could begin to fashion a modern university and educational system suited to their own needs. A University of the West Indies has yet to be developed which can be in Prime Minister Eric Williams' terms "a truly progressive and modern university . . . responsible ideologically for the orientation of the entire educational system in harmony with the needs and aspirations of the people."

In all three of the areas considered within the black world community, black institutions of higher education grew out of post-slavery colonial patterns of educational development. In all three areas, missionary societies and governmental action were the initial forces, usually on a pre-college level. Gradually, college level education was offered, but without status, authority, or support sufficient to justify the term "university." More often than not, there was very little participation by black people in the planning, financing, or decision-making processes. Therefore, the institutions usually fulfilled the traditional functions of teaching and research. Minimal effort went into the development of the communal service aspect of institutional development. Naturally then, the black institutions of higher learning, like the European and American traditional models after which they were fashioned, tended to become disjoined from their surrounding communities (although black colleges and universities have in general been less guilty of this institutional withdrawal than others). Most graduates of black universities were considered to be "elites" by the vast majority of black people. These are the harsh historical realities of most black institutions of higher education throughout the black world community.

It is hoped that this cursory view of the development of some major black universities reveals the intricate pattern of educational exploitation. Only from a black perspective of history can we hope to gain sufficient insight and understanding concerning the present state of institutions of higher education within the black world community.

Purpose of a Black University

We realize now that most "educational matters" are resolved within an economic and political context. Moving from a colonial pattern of university education to an independent pattern directed toward the real needs of people in the black world community is not a simple task. It involves among other things a new institutional purpose, conceptualization, and approach to teaching in all fields, especially in the social sciences. It means we have to begin selecting real everyday problems of people in the black world community as research topics. Finally, it means our definition of community service must correspond with the felt needs and expressed opinions of the people of the black world community.

In order to gain a reorientation—that is to move toward a new perspective of black institutions of higher education—it is necessary to view education within a worldwide economic and political framework. Indeed, we will have to develop a new appreciation of education, especially as it relates to the problems of developing societies. It has been argued that in developing societies all levels of the educational system are parts of the socialization process, and, as such, help transmit the culture and define membership in the society. Within most developing societies, the political argument is seldom centered around the purpose of the university from the standpoint of its teaching and research functions. More likely than not, the debate turns on the question of the social responsibility of the university as an institution within the society.

There are some opinions of black scholars from developing societies which point the way toward a more socially responsible role for the university in developing societies. Their viewpoints suggest to me that the black university can be defined in a manner that allows harmony to replace a "state of tension." Their views suggest the possibility that in the black world community it is possible for black politicians and educators to harmonize their respective roles. Both roles are essential. The task of black political leadership is to govern and maintain viable black political communities; black educational leadership must seek to develop whole black men capable of making a black political community worthy of free men.

Dr. Bernard Fonlon, a Cameroonian scholar-politician, has argued in his essay "The Idea of Culture" that an educational system derives its purpose from its culture; thus the kind of man a given society wants to produce becomes the end of education. In ancient Africa, he asserts: "The virile man . . . had to be a virtuous man—engaged in war against all his society believed to be wrong." This was the African cultural objective. Consequently, Fonlon claims that the end of a modern African educational system must be to "restore manhood in a race unmanned."

Lloyd Braithwaite, writing on "The Role of the University in the Developing Society of the West Indies," held that the traditional functions of the university—teaching and research —have constituted the framework of much of the debate on the future of universities in developing societies. He urges that "besides teaching and research, we may list as important functions of the university:

    (a) The maintenance of cultural traditions on the higher
        level.

    (b) The development of national cultural patterns.

    (c) An advisory and leadership role in modern society."

Braithwaite suggests that in discussing the role of the university in the developing society, "it is precisely these functions that need to be stressed."

But purpose without a means of achieving it does not lead to a reduction in tension between the university and a developing society. If the important aim of the black university is to "develop men," and in addition, to teach, do research, and be of service, then the question arises how can this best be done? President Julius Nyerere of Tanzania has provided us with some valuable insights. Writing on the practical aspects of Africanizing a colonial school system, he urges the development of education which develops a man's mind and his service capacity. The truly educated man develops his knowledge and skills not only for himself, but also to fulfill his communal responsibilities. He obtains his education in such a manner that he is not only familiar with both urban and rural societies, but he is capable of functioning successfully in both cultures.

Education takes place in a total environment, and both the student and teacher should have a sense of responsibility toward the other people who comprise that environment. Those who know must be willing to teach those who seek to learn. Education, even higher education, for Nyerere is cooperative; its method is communal rather than individualistic and competitive. Educational institutions in developing societies have social purposes which can be in harmony with the traditions of the society. In Africa to be African means to feel a part of the community—to give as well as to receive. Indeed, social responsibility is a "given" in modern African higher education, as the Joint Statement at a recent UNESCO sponsored conference on "The Development of Higher Education in Africa" eloquently testifies:

> . . . in addition to the traditional role of giving a broad liberal education, African universities must reflect the needs of the African world by providing African society with men and women equipped with skills that will enable them to participate fully and usefully in the economic and social development of their continent . . . African institutions of higher education have the duty of acting as instruments for the consolidation of national unity . . .
>
> African institutions of higher education are at once the main instruments of national progress, the chief guardian of the people's heritage and the voice of the people in the international councils of technology and scholarship. This triple role, progressive, conservative and collaborative, is an excitingly challenging one.

Thus, we come to realize that developing a black perspective on higher education requires that we seek to understand the role of the university in developing societies as a frame of reference. For, whether we live in Africa, the Caribbean, or in the United States of America, we black people are in varying stages of the process of modern political and educational development. The common legacy of the past shared by black institutions of higher education suggests the possibility of at least three alternative courses of action toward realization of purpose:

1. To continue along the path originally traced by colonial governments which felt they knew our educational needs.

2. To follow an "enlightened" course based on the social and political realities as interpreted for us by nonblack institutions of higher education.

3. To exercise our right to educational and political self-determination, and move collectively to define for ourselves the significance of higher education from our own perspective—thereby producing a synthesis between knowledge for self and service to the community within a worldwide black university.

Some blacks have rejected the first course out of political and educational necessity. The second alternative for social and economic reasons still dominates the thinking of many black men in positions of responsibility throughout the black world community. But the time has come for all of us to consider the third option—to seek for ourselves a modern synthesis—to develop whole black men. Black universities now are technically able to undertake a serious review of the total educational needs of black communities throughout the world. The question remains: Will we psychologically, politically, and economically undertake such a cooperative effort?

The Black University: A New Model

Education from a black perspective must operate on all levels: primary, secondary, specialized, and the university. Thus, we must begin to think of our education as a total system. The black university has to be a new entity derived from the cooperative labors of individual black scholars, educators, and students within existing black institutions throughout the black world community. The black university must be based on a commitment to further knowledge and research, especially related to needs of the people it serves. We know our needs experientially as well as intellectually. Yet, in order to realize our full potential as men we must know more.

The concept of a black university is necessary to enable us black people to realize ourselves fully in a pluralistic world environment. The concept of the black university will help us as we seek solutions to our practical problems of hunger, malnutrition, disease, poverty, and lack of basic education. Thus, the black university has as its primary mission teaching, research, and service for blacks; and it must begin to determine the true value of the human experience within the black world community. Research in the black university must be about our perception of the problems that confront black people.

We must recognize above all that the aims of the black university can be achieved only with the conscious support and participation of the people.

To accomplish this task we must have a plan—an educational development plan which encompasses all the human and technical resources within the black world community. The detailed conceptualization of this plan must of necessity come from the black university community; but the realization of such a plan depends on our awareness of the politics of education. In any case, an educational development plan must have as its ultimate objective the restoration of black manhood throughout the world.

Some may question the need for such a radical approach to the educational problems of black communities. The truth is, however, that there are compelling forces, operative within our communities, directing our energies toward greater self and communal awareness. The question, therefore, is less one of "should" we move to develop a plan for a black university than "how" can such a plan be developed to ensure positive change.

A plan for the educational and social development of black

people must establish a rational pattern which clearly delineates: (a) a rationale—a new multinational educational theory; (b) specific goals to be achieved; (c) target dates to accomplish the stated objectives; and (d) a process whereby ongoing communication can exist among educational, cultural, religious, economic, and political leadership throughout the black world community.

Our educational development plan must have a theoretical base because "facts come to mean something only as ascertained and organized in the form of a theory." The "triangle theory" is that the black world community exists within a triangular pattern of relationships among black people in Africa, the Caribbean, and the United States. We maintain that the common origins, customs, music, dance, food, and life interests of most of the people in this geographical area constitute, in part, a basis for building a viable community life. Further, we assert that with a new educational perspective—a black perspective—we will come to see that our future social, economic, cultural, and political stability depends upon our efforts to strengthen these ancestral bonds.

To test this theory we will have to develop a black university—a university which is the outgrowth of our efforts to develop a new black perspective on higher education. It need not be in any one physical place; it can be a theoretical model which enables all institutions of higher education throughout the black world community to work cooperatively in developing the "triangle theory." Thus, black universities can take up the challenge by contributing to a fund of knowledge and research directed toward the needs of the people of the black world community.

We must move to accept the challenges inherent in building a new theory for ourselves. The "triangle theory" can guide our attempts to seek the educational and social development of the black world community. It is through the application of this theory that we seek the full realization of our potential human personality. Indeed, the development and application of the "triangle theory" constitute the main challenge facing black people during the second half of this century.

We must begin this important task by calling a series of local and regional meetings. Such discussions should seek a common understanding of the main objectives and a timetable for implementation of a multinational educational development plan. This should be followed by a conference of representatives from all parts of the triangle area to discuss "The Role of the University in the Black World Community." Among other things the participants in such a conference should consider:

1. The establishment of *Regional University Centers* which would coordinate services offered by institutions of higher education throughout a given geographical region within the triangle area (viz., Atlanta University —Institute of the Black World in the United States; University of the West Indies—Institute of Social and Economic Research; and University of Ghana—Institute of African Studies). Such regional centers could then encourage the development of satellite centers throughout their respective regions with similar objectives, by focusing on one or more specific problems facing the people of the region (i.e., special health, nutrition, labor, education, recreation, economic, or social problems). The satellite centers would operate in collaboration with the Regional Center. In the United States, for instance, Atlanta University and the Institute of the Black World might function as a Regional Center, and smaller black educational institutions would function in collaboration on specific problem areas.

2. The utilization of *Regional University Consortia*—to develop within specified geographical areas lines of communication with all levels of the educational system,

thereby increasing opportunities for integration of edu
cational services within the surrounding black com
munities. Through utilization of a systems approach
significant steps could be taken to develop cooperativel
and economically: text books; teaching aids; curricula–
sharing devices, through technological innovation; join
in-service training projects; language institutes, student
faculty exchanges, and a host of other cooperative con
tacts.

3. The creation of a *Black Educational Service.* Educa
tional leaders could meet locally, regionally, and inter
nationally on an annual or biannual basis in variou
parts of the black world, to discuss ways and means o
furthering their collaborative efforts. Such a grou
could serve as a resource to institutions attempting t
develop new programs.

4. The establishment of *Libraries and Community De
velopment Centers* through the cooperation of blac
institutions of higher education and the people of blac
communities in all parts of the black world. Such cen
ters could be located in black communities and name
in honor of black heroes whose work might be carrie
on through the operations of these centers and libraries
Such centers and libraries could be dedicated to th
preservation, appreciation, and development of th
ideas of such men as Du Bois of the United States
Garvey of the Caribbean, and Nkrumah of Africa.

It is obvious that a planned system of education—multi
national in character—can ultimately reach each and ever
individual in the black world community. No lesser goa
is realistic if we hope to give real meaning to the term
"brother." Although the developing societies worldwide ar
undergoing rapid technological change and urbanization, th
fact remains that "some two-thirds of the world's childre
live in rural areas . . . and most of the world's rural chi

dren receive no schooling at all." Ultimately, the needs of these "brothers" are the real objects of any plans we suggest for educational change.

The historical experience of blacks in Africa, America, and the Caribbean reveals very similar patterns of educational colonization. This experience points up the need for a new perspective—a black perspective of the purpose and functions of institutions of higher education in black communities. This new perspective will enable us to begin formulating a development plan, a blueprint for the conceptualization of a unique university—a black university—a university that will teach and contribute to world knowledge through research for and about black people. But it can do more! The black university envisioned will help free our children and prepare them for manhood in a new world community. It seeks to build a new educational model—one that is pro-black, not anti-white. Its purpose is positive. The concept of a black university can be our unique contribution to a new world order where manhood is possible for all at the expense of none.

We black educators, scholars, and students must pledge to work toward a black university in repayment of our debt to the black world community which gave us life and a sense of purpose. Our efforts will help to ensure that future generations of educated black men and women will not need to "return to their communities." Through the black university they will have learned the meaning of living, learning, and serving within a worldwide black community. Then, and only then, can we fulfill the difficult task of education that is still ahead of us.

2

Black Studies: Is a Valid Idea Being Invalidated?

by Jim Haskins

Mr. Haskins is the author of Diary of a Harlem School-teacher; Resistance: Profiles in Nonviolence; Revolutionaries: Agents of Change; The War and the Protest: Vietnam; Profiles in Black Power; A Piece of the Power: Four Black Mayors, *and is co-author, with Hugh F. Butts, M.D., of* The Psychology of Black Language. *His articles include "Where Poverty is Total"* (Together *magazine, June 1970*), *"Sesame Street"* (Tuesday *magazine, August 1970*), *"Black Studies: A Valid Idea Invalidated?"* (Urban Review of Black Writing, *Spring 1972*) *and "The Proper School for the Proper Negro"* (Contact *magazine, February 1972*). *He is a professor in the Experimental College Program at Staten Island Community College. Mr. Haskins lives in New York City.*

The concept of black studies programs is a valid and realistic one. An outgrowth of the new emphasis upon black pride and self-awareness, that concept deals directly with the indisputable fact that history has been whitewashed and that the black experience has, for the most part, been ignored. The arena for the black studies controversy is the predominantly white university. Negro colleges and universities already stress black history and culture; students attending these institutions are usually well versed in black studies. Black students attending predominantly white schools, on the other hand, feel understandably that they are in an alien world, surrounded by whites and learning almost exclusively white history and culture. They seek more relevant curricula in their academic lives. Others seek relevance with respect to the work they eventually plan to do in the black community; they feel that black studies will provide them with additional tools to carry back to the black community.

Not a primary but perhaps an implicit objective in seeking black studies in white universities is that white students will also have the opportunity to become aware of the black heritage and thus to gain a better understanding of the black experience. Whites, too, have suffered from the intellectual imbalance which has resulted from the neglect of black history and culture. Steps have to be taken to redress that intellectual imbalance, and the originators of the black studies concept rightly perceive that this redress could never occur through existing courses. Available textbooks do not deal with black contributions in any more than a cursory manner, and all professors cannot be counted upon to incorporate sufficient additional material on blacks into their courses. The proper mode of redress, then, is the creation of courses devoted exclusively to black subjects.

At this point, the concept of black studies is on solid ground: The need for black studies is indisputable, the embryonic program appears workable, its objectives are beneficial. But many of those who have sought to make the concept a reality and to implement the program have become confused about or have rejected most of the original objectives. The problems range from faculty selection to whether or not to allow white students to enroll in the courses. The latter problem is particularly crucial, for inherent in it are questions not only of legality but also of the real moral and educational existence of the university itself.

The university has always existed as a forum for free intellectual discussion of ideas of all shapes and colors. Many times it has come under pressure from individuals and groups who have tried to force it to modify its self-concept. That is not to say that change and modification are bad; in certain isolated situations revolution is desirable. But many revolutionary movements on our college campuses, although they begin with agitation for valid changes, become bogged down in confusion over issues that either did not exist or were of minor importance when the agitation began. The free speech movement at Berkeley was valid and serious when it began, for it agitated for the right of all people, whatever their political persuasion (including blacks) to speak on the campus. But the issues became clouded, and soon there were demands for the full range of free expression, including obscenity, the aspect that of course got the widest possible media coverage. And of course the officials sought to discredit the whole movement purely on the basis of profanity and obscenity. Unfortunately, a similar fate seems to be in store for the black studies movement. The many legitimate and valuable aspects are being overshadowed by the issues of separatism and black student control of the black studies programs.

The whole gestalt, of course, is the historical truth that black people have been forced, or perhaps one should say tricked, into being voiceless and childish. Thus, now that we have come of age as a result of black power (whatever that means, and it does suggest many things from the standpoint of growth) we must assert our manhood in various ways. The black youth in the universities assert their manhood through force-pressure to make the universities offer courses in black studies. Okay, that's good; that's black power. That's also good economics, for it enables a few official blacks, who otherwise might not have gotten there alone, to get jobs at the universities.

But what about those few white students who barricade

themselves inside administration buildings with black students, smuggle in sandwiches, or otherwise aid black students to gain black studies programs? These white students help because they realize they know nothing about the cultural existence of blacks in America, not to mention Africa, and they know that it is wrong not to know about them. They know of black misery in America and of black and brown misery in the so-called Third World, and they want to help. And there are probably many more who would help if it were not for the constant atmosphere of danger and violence that surrounds every confrontation and building takeover on campuses around the country. What about the white students? When it is all over and the dry, dull little men in their vested suits have capitulated, black students have often tried to expel their white counterparts and any other whites who may be interested in hearing what has to be taught in black studies from the new courses.

It all seems a sort of rhetorical nightmare. Black kids want separate dormitories because they say white kids don't understand them, but they won't allow the white kids into the one course or program that might define for them what black confusion or consciousness is all about in the first place.

If we attempt to understand the problem in the light of this sort of unconscious double-talk or the cineramic drama that we occasionally see on television during coverage of black student takeovers of university buildings, the nightmare will persist. What we have to do is look at the whole problem from a psychological standpoint. Behind black students' attempts to bar white students from black studies courses is frustration and confusion over their own identity, expressed through rage, destruction of property, and sometimes guns and bare masculine courage. This is probably why black students object to white students in the black studies courses. Black students have read Ralph Ellison's *Invisible Man* and have seen part of themselves in it. Invisibility suggests a lack of identity with the self. If this is the case for the exclusion of whites, then it is legitimate. But perhaps instead of insisting upon black studies they should insist upon black analysis conducted by black psychiatrists, because unless they can criticize themselves they will never be brave enough to admit their invisibility.

Unfortunately, many black studies programs have indeed come to concentrate upon black analysis or black solidarity against whites rather than upon black academics. Many of these programs have combined academics with counseling programs, separate social facilities, and community action programs, to the obvious detriment of the academic aspect. And even the academic courses often stress solidarity and common identity rather than learning. Soon after "Racism in America," an experimental course at Berkeley that was open to both white and black students, began, the black students complained that they were being used as resource persons.

An exclusively black section of the course was then set up and a black psychiatrist chosen to teach it. The result was a course with no required reading and no other class work besides, as some students described it, "bull sessions," where they "got down on whitey." These students either were not secure enough to interact with white students in a class on racism or they were not interested in helping the white students understand racism. In a separate section, they were not sufficiently open-minded to admit that they did not know all about racism and that the academic study of it might have yielded increased understanding. It would seem that if these students all understood racism, then there is no need for them to take black sociology courses, although such courses are in great demand. An academic format is not necessary for bull sessions; in fact it is wasted when utilized for that purpose.

It is understandable that black students should be hyper

sensitive to any attempted exploitation by white students in integrated black studies courses. It is also understandable that black students' frustration over their invisibility should take the form of insistence upon exclusion of whites. It is true that by excluding whites, black students not only become isolated and thereby confirm themselves as individuals but also make whites aware that they too can be invisible in the eyes of blacks. Hopefully, the whites are relating this minor experience of invisibility to the black experience of exclusion and invisibility in American history. But white understanding of blacks' historical invisibility can be brought about in a much more constructive manner—by allowing white students to take black studies courses. It would seem that students, black and white, would benefit greatly from such a mutual learning situation if they could regard it as such rather than as a mutually competitive, exploitative situation. In addition, black pride would be enhanced through interaction with whites in an area in which the black students have the greater expertise. Finally, it is naïve to think that white institutions will continue to provide or even initiate quality educational programs that exclude whites.

Black students who desire to exclude whites from their programs demonstrate their own confusion and are actually reversing the original priorities of the black studies concept. Emotional needs have taken precedence over intellectual needs. This shift of priorities is further manifested in the material that black students choose to include in black studies courses. Very often, the subjects and personalities chosen to study are those which serve to reinforce their own self-image or militancy. As the greatest outcropping of militant ideas and personalities is occurring at the present time, the consequence is a historicity. Such figures as Nat Turner and Marcus Garvey are usually included, for example, in black history courses, but to understand black history (to appreciate it) black students must read John Hope Franklin,

E. Franklin Frazier, Saunders Redding, Vincent Harding, Benjamin Quarles, Du Bois, and the many other thinkers in the black American cultural heritage who spent their lives gathering and researching the information which has made the study of black history possible, who devoted themselves to scholarship rather than to rhetoric. Malcolm X and LeRoi Jones are valid too, but in the contexts of autobiography and poetry, which are reality and creative genius, not history.

The black studies concept is new, and it takes time to search out what is relevant to the concept. An overemphasis upon contemporary problems and personalities, however, hinders the discovery of relevant material in the past. The general rule of thumb in college courses with a historical orientation has been to study the past in relation to the present. It is expected that students who are interested in the particular subject will keep abreast of contemporary events relative to that subject on their own. Political science courses do not deal in depth with, for example, the Nixon administration; contemporary politics are debated as an adjunct to the curriculum rather than taught per se. An overemphasis upon contemporary events in black studies courses will not equip students to propose new solutions to the problems which have and continue to beset the black existence in America.

At the other end of the spectrum from black studies programs that are relevant only to contemporary problems are the courses that are so insipid as to be irrelevant in any real sense. Such courses as "The Selection and Preparation of Soul Food" and "The Sociology of Black Sports"—as separate courses—are relevant in that they satisfy emotional needs, but their intellectual relevancy is debatable. In choosing the material for black studies courses the emphasis should be upon quality rather than quantity. Every single element of the black experience could conceivably be treated as a separate course, but by thus isolating these elements from each other and from any larger context those who structure black studies programs structure in an intellectual shallowness of which the students will soon tire.

In addition, a black studies course should be as difficult as any other course on campus. Failure to require high standards of performance in these courses can only serve to discredit them. They must not become institutionalized bull sessions. Required reading and learning dates and material by rote is purposeful, for these methods reinforce the material in the mind. Neither learning by rote nor studying the scholars serves to reinforce the self-concept of the black students who scoff at such material and methods. But no relevant and responsible black studies program can afford to ignore the time-tested methods of learning that characterize a meaningful learning situation. These time-tested methods are also coming under fire from many white students; however, protest against proven methodology is only tangential to protest against irrelevancy. In this context, black studies courses have the potential to become some of the most meaningful courses on college campuses—for white students as well as black students. The current protest by white students against irrelevancy in their academic lives centers around the humanities, particularly literature, history, and sociology. It is in these academic areas that neglect of large segments of the subject matter—black contributions and the black experience—has the most tragic implications in the context of student alienation. By offering these neglected segments within the existing academic framework, black studies programs can contribute greatly to resolving the crises in relevancy that affect many college campuses.

The entire campus community could benefit also from the influx of qualified teachers, if their knowledge and teaching abilities are not restricted entirely to separate and segregated black studies programs. This benefit will be derived, however, by the population of predominantly white universities at the expense of black institutions, at least until a larger pool of qualified black teachers is available. The inception of black studies programs and black students' demands for black professors have caused problems that have assumed crisis proportions in the country's black universities. Having nowhere else to turn for qualified black professors, the white universities are raiding the faculties of the good black universities. Thus the black students are undermining the black schools for the sake of achieving separation on the white campuses. A bit incomprehensible, isn't it?

The demand that only black professors teach black studies courses also runs the risk of relegating black professors solely to the field of black studies, isolating and restricting what they may teach. A black authority on black literature may also be an authority on literature in general or on Hemingway or Faulkner. It is unfair to both the professor and the university to isolate him and prevent him from becoming an asset to the university in general.

Finally, black students must put to responsible use their newly acquired voice in the selection of black studies faculty members. Rigid insistence upon only black professors is self-defeating. If the demand is really for scholarship and expertise, then there certainly are a number of qualified and morally acceptable whites who satisfy those requirements. Also, in choosing black teachers, consideration of political views must not take precedence over consideration of academic qualifications. Unfortunately, black students tend to reject many black candidates for teaching positions simply on the basis that the candidates are not sufficiently militant or nationalistic. Such a tendency is dangerous to intellectual freedom, for there can be no meaningful intellectual dialogue between people whose ideas are the same.

Many of the foregoing problems spring from a common source—the politicalization of the black studies concept. Although it was probably inevitable, politicalization is perhaps the most unfortunate development in the black studies controversy. That is not to suggest that politics has no place in the university; all things are political, but to varying degrees. The concept of politics coming out of the barrel of a gun should not be applied to the politics of a university. Because it has been applied to the black studies controversy, that controversy has often been used as an arena for the sometimes gladiatorial struggles between different black power and black nationalist groups. It is no accident that two members of the Black Panther party who were students at UCLA were shot in the UCLA lunchroom in January, 1969, allegedly by members of Karenga's US during a struggle for control of the Afro-American Studies Center there.

Politicalization has caused the nationalist concept of American black people as a colony within the borders of the white mother country to be carried over to the university, where what the nationalists seek are separate black enclaves within the white institutions. As some nationalists demand that the mother country give them a "land base" of three or four Southern states, so they demand that the white mother universities give black students what Theodore Draper writing in the September, 1969, issue of *Commentary* has called "ersatz foreign institutions with extraterritorial rights." While the white mother country has thus far ignored the former demand, the white mother university has capitulated with amazing rapidity. It is the reaction of the white universities to black student demands that constitutes perhaps the most sinister aspect of the black studies controversy—sinister not only for the black students but also in the context of the long-espoused moral and educational responsibilities of the university.

Black students must really analyze whether or not colleges and universities are sincere when they create black studies programs. It is clear to many people that some colleges and universities give in to demands for black studies thinking that "the fad will die out soon." Still others have deliberately organized ill-conceived programs because they are intended only for black students. It is almost like segregated schools; you can get the best education in an integrated setting. When a white university bows to demands for separate black studies programs and faculties it is in effect doing exactly what black students have accused it of doing all the while. In this context, however, the university is hailed instead of indicted as racist: acceding to racism in reverse and getting a medal for it. Inadvertently or willingly, white colleges are reinforcing apartheid in America. Black students who are inordinately sensitive to exploitation and racism by white universities in other areas seem strangely naïve in trusting white institutions to give them quality segregated black studies programs.

All of these problems give rise to the question of the value and relevancy of the black studies major to the needs of black students. Given that at least some institutions have deliberately organized weak black studies programs, what value will a degree in black studies from these institutions have for the students who wish to pursue their education further? For those students who intend to work in the black community after graduation, will expertise in black studies be more helpful than expertise in business, law, communications? Finally, will majoring in black studies adequately prepare the black student to deal effectively and knowledgeably with white society? The goal of inclusion of black studies programs into university curricula is, of course, most immediate. But one must look further than the goal of inclusion; one has to consider long-range objectives.

The foregoing problems indeed place the whole concept of black studies in jeopardy. But these problems can be overcome if black students and the universities can seriously consider and acknowledge certain facts. First, that black studies could be a highly successful and exciting addition to the life of any university if proposed and implemented correctly. Second, that it is wrong and self-defeating to isolate black studies programs from white students and professors and thus from the university in general. And finally, that despite the communications media's encouraged tendency to view the black students at Harvard, San Francisco State, and Columbia as spokesmen for the black student movement, the majority of black students enrolled at white colleges and universities have not rejected the original purpose of the black studies concept. In this context, a letter written by a black student to one of the Yale administrators during the crisis there is encouraging:

> We do not [he wrote] talk of black studies here. We do speak of an Afro-American Program, which we define as an American Studies Curriculum which structures into the corpus of historical and literary material the substantive facts about black Americans . . . Our argument is that the course in American history that ignores or slights the black man's role is a bad course. We believe that writing by black Americans is American writing, and that to segregate it from the body of American expression is a ridiculous exercise of ignorance, and that it does great harm to American literature as an instrument of cultural and aesthetic diagnosis . . .

3

Curriculum Changes for Freshman English Programs in the Black College

by Alma S. Freeman

Miss Freeman was born in Alabama, where she received her public school and undergraduate college education. For a number of years she taught English in the public school systems of Alabama and at Alabama State University. She received the M.A. degree in English from Ohio State University and is presently studying for the Ed.D. degree in English Education at Rutgers University. She is a member of the National Council of Teachers of English, Delta Sigma Theta sorority, and Alpha Kappa Mu, national honor society. In March, 1972, she delivered a paper to a special interest group at the Conference on College Composition and Communication in Boston on teaching freshman English in the Black College.

In the *Harvard Educational Review* in 1967, David Riesman and Christopher Jencks pronounced the sentence of execution. A year later, Nathan Hare followed with firsthand evidence in the *Saturday Review* to support, confirm, and applaud their decision. Yet, despite the claims of educational incompetence, the pressures of racial integration, the pains of insufficient finances, and the drains on qualified faculty and personnel, the black college struggled for survival. Many in educational circles questioned the endurance of black edu-

128

cation in the face of such adversity. But if the decade of the sixties ended with a proclamation of death for the black college, it also closed with the emergence of a new black consciousness which refocused attention on keeping the black college alive and viable. And the decade of the seventies opened with increased numbers of black educators protesting the demise of black education, affirming its value for the black community, but calling for a redirection of its efforts—a reevaluation of its purpose and its role in light of the new black awareness. These appeals by black educators, along with increased federal funding for selected black institutions and the $100 million Ford Foundation grant to ten private black colleges, symbolize a new realism in dealing with a much neglected sector of higher education and in providing a more meaningful educational experience for the hundreds of thousands of black youths demanding cultural relevance. Apparently, then, the death sentence has been lifted for many black colleges.

Today, therefore, the problem facing the black college is no longer one of survival; change is now the crucial issue confronting predominantly black institutions. Black people are expressing a growing dissatisfaction with the methods of their colleges whose programs imitate those of white institutions and aim at educating solely for mainstream living. Realizing that few blacks really make the mainstream, black Americans are demanding that their colleges be more responsive to their needs and aspirations as black people, that they also educate for an understanding of blackness and of what this means in America. Thus, if the black college is to serve black people effectively and answer the demands of today's black youth, its future role must be a dual one: The black college must develop curricula that will prepare black youth for effective participation in the larger American society—for competition in an economy undergoing dramatic changes in the demand for skills. At the same time, these curricula must be designed to help students see clearly and understand fully the true position of black people in American society, prepare them to deal intelligently with the social and economic oppression they must inevitably face, and help them acquire intellectual strategies for engineering social change.

Those of us responsible for curriculum development and instruction in the freshman English programs of these schools find ourselves faced with pertinent questions: How can freshman English aid the black college in fulfilling its dual responsibility? What should freshman English do for the new generation of black students? Our main purpose here is to suggest some answers to these questions and to make recommendations for curriculum changes in the freshman English program in light of the newly defined role and purpose of the black college.

Clearly, freshman English as it has existed in most black colleges fails to meet the needs of the black student. In fact, many freshman English courses cause the student to experience defeat before he really begins. The moment the student enters the classroom, he encounters a barrage of theme assignments thrown at him by a teacher sheltered behind a podium. He then wrestles with literary models by sophisticated, usually white, essayists selected for use as patterns for his themes. At some point, he struggles through drills and exercises on grammar, spelling, punctuation, correct usage, and sentence construction. And he listens (or does not listen) to lectures on style, logic, rhetoric—on symbols, images, and structure, all of which seem quite foreign to him. Constantly reminded that he has entered college behind, he is subjected to a spoon-feeding operation designed to *tell* him all the facts, all he needs to know to "catch up." He thus finds himself locked into the passive role of soaking up information and his learning activity confined to a regurgitation of the facts the teacher has spit out. In such a situation, the student either fails the course or drops out of college; he either learns to give the teacher exactly what he wants (if capable), or he learns to "eat cheese" or to do some "apple polishing" to get by. To be sure, only the strong (in academics or in ego) survive. In any event, original thought and creative production on the student's part are destroyed rather than developed; and the student as person, as human being, is ignored. Without the development of originality, creativity, and a sense of self awareness and self worth, how can students equip themselves to cope with the demands of society?

In the course of his education, a student should acquire more than skills and knowledge. He should also find and continue to modify his image of himself and to shape his attitudes toward the world. Too often, the image mirrored to one is the image he becomes. And because the images constantly mirrored to the black student have been negative ones—roles and stereotypes devoid of humanity—he needs a new looking-glass image that shows self-confidence, self-reliance, and what it means to *be someone,* an image that will provide the thrust to go beyond physical and psychological oppression. Thus the black student does not need to sit back and absorb information *about* language; he needs to use it to talk about his identity, his relationship to society—his life! If freshman English is to aid the college effectively in fulfilling its responsibility to the student, it must operate out of a curriculum designed to help the student in his quest for identity and for an understanding of the world as well as facilitate his mastery of skills and his acquisition of facts. To accomplish this end, faculties must move away from such constrictions of tradition as the teacher-centered classroom which provides no student-to-student or student-to-teacher interaction; the presentation of experience as given through literature, ignoring the personal culture of the student in light of which he reads literature; neglecting the integrity and importance of the student's everyday activities and experiences as integral components of language learning; and many other unwarranted and obsolete approaches to English teaching. Thus the traditional goals, style, and program of instruction must change.

Although the present trend in many American colleges and universities is to discard the freshman English requirement altogether, the black college needs the freshman English course, but not *just* because many black students have language problems that need attention. This, we believe, is secondary to and a part of the students' growth and development as individuals and their use of language to serve this end.

Thus, one main goal of the freshman English course should be to furnish a place where the students can encounter literature relevant to their needs as individuals to help broaden and extend their experiences and thereby contribute to their development of insights into modes of human existence and patterns of social change. The students should be exposed to a variety of literature—poems, plays, essays, novels, short stories, biographies, autobiographies—by black and other ethnic writers as well as white, contemporary as well as traditional. Much of the literature should be selected after the students' interests are known; the students should assist in these selections; and the teacher should be prepared to direct a particular student to readings that relate to the student's own individual interests and experiences. Of necessity, much of the literature should derive from the black experience. If teachers of black students would approach conventional disciplines from the perspective of black culture, they would furnish the student with a familiar groundwork so that he can bring his own knowledge and experience into the life of the classroom. The student would thus obtain a greater degree of personal involvement in the learning process. Our own experiences have shown that black students express greater interest, respond more enthusiastically, and learn more rapidly when we use materials by and about black people as the center of classroom discussions and activities. Each student is able to relate some facet of his own experience to that of the authors he is reading and is anxious to explore and compare these experiences. Thus feeling a sense of personal involvement and commitment, the student does not withdraw from the life of the classroom as readily as he does when all materials used are somewhat foreign to his own life.

When dealing with literature in the classroom, teachers and students in freshman English courses should remember that their concern is with literature and not with literary criticism. The teacher must keep in mind that literature is to be used to give the students a deeper vision of life and aid them in formulating their own views, in making their own judgments. Many black students do not like literature because they are always talked to about form and technique. The life and the experience as embodied in the literary work get glossed over and the author's aesthetics become all-important. Black students do not need to sit back and look at structure, symbols, and images. They have more to worry about—life! If literature is to help the student come to grips with the problems of life, therefore, the teacher must focus on the content, the life, and the experience in the literary work rather than on form and technique. Surely literature is one way of acquiring a new vision of life. It can enable students to gain perceptions for themselves. Hence, students must be encouraged to analyze, question, and challenge certain assumptions about life and about human behavior in literary works, to explore the fullness of the author's vision and judge his partialities and prejudices. They must be made to realize that structure, symbols, and images are merely tools for expressing larger issues, that these are a means and not an end in themselves. Through this kind of analysis of literature, students can gain a new awareness of life—learn how things are, why they are this way, and how they can be different. They can see a need for improvement and develop the will, the courage, and perhaps the means for effecting personal and social change.

When encounters occur in literary works with representations of blacks and other minority groups that are demeaning, insensitive, or unflattering to the culture, for instance, the class should discuss why this has happened and how it could be different. Consider Mark Twain's *The Adventures of Huckleberry Finn,* for example. Especially at the beginning and at the end of the novel, Twain represents Jim as a minstrel-show figure, a stereotype stripped of humanity, and he makes the relationship between Huck and Jim essentially demeaning. At other points, Twain portrays Jim as a sensitive human being and as a spiritual father to Huck. Students should be encouraged to analyze this ambivalence in character portrayal and discuss why it exists in terms of the social circumstances surrounding the novel and Twain's ambivalence toward slavery. In addition to Jim, they should be encouraged to look at Pap Finn and the educated black college professor who speaks six languages. They should also explore the novel's expression of freedom. Consider also Joseph Conrad's *Heart of Darkness.* Rather than focus in an isolated fashion on Conrad's use of light and dark images to show the black-white contrast in the novel, for instance, the class should use these to analyze and explore the duality in Conrad's attitude toward blacks, the evils of oppression and exploitation, and the greed and selfishness that underlie the trading companies' humanitarian pretenses in the heart of Africa.

The black college freshman is an individual on the verge of maturity facing choices in a largely racist society. Literature, if used effectively, can be a valuable aid in clarifying his understanding of the black experience, the American experience, and the larger human experience as well. It can thus provide insights into the possible choices open to him and force an awareness of the necessity of positive action rather than complacent passivity if any change in social conditions is to be effected. It can further make him realize the necessity of channeling his actions in the right direction. Works of fiction which express the theme of adolescent initiation and growth are especially valuable. Mark Twain's *The Adventures of Huckleberry Finn* and Ralph Ellison's *Invisible Man* provide good examples. Each novel portrays its young protagonist encountering experiences from which he learns that hypocrisy is inherent in society's behavior. Each novel declares that basic human rights must be defended despite the attitudes and fears generated in a hypocritical, racist milieu. Both Huck and the hero of *Invisible Man* face moral choices. Huck must decide whether or not to free the slave Jim. In freeing Jim, he accepts a moral and personal responsibility in the condition of society. The hero of *Invisible Man,* retiring in his home underground, must examine the meaning of his experiences and decide whether to be active in or remain a recluse from society. A black adolescent who once embraced faith in the system, the invisible man is ultimately stripped of illusion. Through his varied roles, he has acted out opposing strategies of being for society or against it. The new vision born of his conflicts allows him to embrace the complexity of his life and at the same time retain hope that he, as an individual, as a human being, can take an active part in this society. Now isolated from the brutal world, more intelligent and more mature, he is aware of his social responsibility and decides that he must return to society to work diligently and shrewdly to improve the black man's plight and through extension, the human condition.

Similarly, Richard Wright's *Native Son* presents a black youth confronting a repressive society. Here, Wright pictures Bigger Thomas, a brutal, sullen, and arrogant young man, who sincerely desires to participate in society as a human being without the limitations or set patterns of life which the order forces him to pursue. Bigger merely wants to establish the human link that he feels should rationally exist between men exclusive of racial and other barriers. He resents other blacks for quietly accepting their misery and their exclusion from the wider society, and for their resignation to being assigned to an inferior status. Their path, he feels, cannot be his. Like Twain's Huck Finn and Ellison's invisible man, therefore, Bigger makes a choice. He chooses rebellion and violence and thereby gains an identity for himself. Though he is labeled a beast, a monster, he prefers this identity to passive submission and acquiescence to exploitation. He at least acts and accepts responsibility for his actions; he asserts his humanity and acquires a measure of freedom and manhood. Though Bigger chooses this direction and gains a sense of being in and a part of the world, he realizes that he has found no real solutions; for while he, for the first time, feels alive, his acts of violence have only more securely alienated him from mankind and further destroyed the possibility of establishing meaningful lines of communication with others. To show Wright's contrasting view, "The Man Who Lived Underground" may be placed beside *Native Son*. While Bigger Thomas' rebellious violence gains him his identity, Fred Daniels, the hero of "The Man Who Lived Underground," realizes that he must come to grips with an absurd world and make the most of it by working within the system for human improvement. He achieves his identity only when his experiences underground convince him both that it is futile to expect to find meaning in an irrational world and that he must accept his social responsibility despite the absurdity of human existence.

Ellison's *Invisible Man* and Wright's *Native Son* may also lead into discussions of roles and categories imposed by society—of class, ethnic, and sex distinctions as well as racial differences that lock people into oppressive roles, drain their vitality, and stifle their full growth as human beings. Such discussions may lead to the question of why should roles exist and to considerations of possible ways of breaking down stereotypes, roles, and categories and seeing others as human beings.

Like Ellison's invisible man, Marlow in Conrad's *Heart of Darkness* looks back on his experiences which served as his introduction to the adult world. Marlow's journey to the Congo is an initiation into a fuller scale of human being, and it brings him a feeling of growth and of fuller participation in the human condition. Through his observations of Kurtz, for example, Marlow makes a discovery about himself and about all men. Away from society which provides controls in its rules, regulations, laws, and taboos, Kurtz discovers that he is free to be, to do, anything—good or evil. But he so perverts this freedom, this knowledge of being human, that he becomes inhuman. He does not evaluate what being free and human really means. Marlow, however, finds value in Kurtz's behavior because Kurtz does throw himself into action. Though he chooses evil, Kurtz makes a commitment, a human choice. At the same time, though, Marlow realizes that not simply one man, but all men, deprived of the insulation of society, may become evil. *Heart of Darkness* thus reveals what happens to a man, the direction he may choose, when free of imposed social codes if he does not respect or take responsibility for the humanity of others.

Such works as T. S. Eliot's "The Love Song of J. Alfred Prufrock" reveal the torment, the frustration, and the emotional conflict that a person endures because of his inability to act on the basis of his feelings and perceptions. Prufrock's natural human feelings and instincts are limited or restricted by social decorum. Thus stifled by his social environment, Prufrock seeks to rebel against his situation but fails because of his own weakness and indecisiveness. Caught up in the barrenness and futility of his own existence, he, though aware of the emptiness of his life, refrains from accepting any responsibility for change. He thus chooses to be the passive individual and remains impotent against the strictures of society. Students may explore possible choices open to Prufrock and the consequences had he chosen to break the barriers of social decorum that confine him and smother his capacity for action, for freeing his native humanity.

The preceding illustrations represent possible ways of looking at literary works to give students deeper insights into human existence and into modes of human behavior. The student learns that many possible choices exist for the individual, but the burden is his to decide which route to take. He also sees that action is necessary if change is to occur, but this action must be properly channeled, that one must retain faith in humanity and respect for the life and rights of others as human beings. Only this kind of directed action can bring personal fulfillment, some measure of happiness, and serve to improve the human condition.

In addition to furnishing the student relevant literature that will aid in his personal growth, the freshman course should provide a student-centered language community where the students and the teacher meet through their own best strengths—their experiences, their ideas, their concept of themselves, and their language—to share their encounters with life, to talk, to write, to read, and in the process find something that will give order to their own individual worlds. One look at our modern technological society reveals a certain paralysis in human relationships. Individuals are unable to talk with each other, to relate to one another in any meaningful way. Through providing a climate for sharing and discussing personal experiences and ideas, freshman English can enable students to establish effective lines of communication with each other that, it is hoped, will extend into the college family and into the community and aid in

breaking down barriers that thwart effective human inter-
course.

If a student is to seek equality in society, he should experience this equality in the microcosmic world of the classroom. Especially in the black college does the teacher usually
demand distance and respect on the basis of his position.
He is the absolute dictator who requires instant and unques-
tioning obedience. This traditional student-teacher barrier
must be broken if the student is to feel that he and the
teacher are engaged in a common enterprise, that he is receiving knowledge because it is attractive to him instead of
having it imposed or forced upon him. In order that this
kind of learning can take place, the classroom environment
must be conducive to personal interaction and to the free
flow of ideas. Such an environment must be free of the au-
thoritative pressures of the conventional college classroom.
Thus a student-centered or open classroom situation would
prove more effective. This would de-emphasize the teacher's
role as authority figure and information giver and emphasize
the student's role as active participant and equal sharer in
the learning process. The teacher's role would become that
of flexible planner, resource person, and informal director
and also participant in activities.

In such a classroom environment, the creative, imaginative
teacher can devise numerous instructional techniques to find
the most effective means of reaching students, "turning them
on," and thus provide for their individual differences. Many
teachers talk about individual differences but continue to
use uniform books, administer standard examinations, use
seating charts, and give the same theme assignments that they
feel have worked well in the past. If a student is to know he
is being treated in a personal manner, such standard measures
should be avoided. Students bring to the classroom differences
of background, interests, and capabilities; thus each student

can be a valuable resource person, that is, if the teacher is not afraid of spirited discussions and heated debates. Such activities enable students to feel that the classroom is theirs as well as the teacher's. Discussion and small group interaction, therefore, should be an essential part of the life of the classroom. This, however, does not mean the usual kind of class discussion consisting of questions from the teacher and answers from one student at a time. The teacher should encourage honest student-to-student interaction in an effort to help students learn from each other. Perhaps the best way to effect this is to abolish hand raising and recognition by the teacher, but maintain a rule of not interrupting and of respecting what another has to say. During discussions, the teacher should encourage the expansion of dialogue through questioning, elaborating, amending, and providing evidence —the same process followed in thinking and writing. The student will thus transform these processes internally into his normal modes of thought. When the class divides into small groups for some activity, the teacher should rotate from group to group acting as consultant and joining the discussions. Individual students should be induced to detach from the group, at times, and talk alone. They may read their compositions, summarize discussions, relate narrative experiences, or give "how-to" talks. Significantly, feedback from the class should be encouraged. Topics for writing should spring from such discussions. At some point, students should be encouraged to write their own literature—stories, poems, plays, and so forth—and to share it with each other. They may also keep weekly journals or diaries of any kind of writing they would like to do. Class time should be devoted to free writing activities. These should not be graded or corrected but may be read and discussed by the class or small groups if a student has no objections. Such activities stimulate individual expression and provide constant practice in writing.

Since the content for the course will derive from the students' interests and experiences, from reading materials relevant to these and to the students' needs and aspirations as black people, and from the students' writing, some effective means must be devised for getting these into the life of the classroom. Improvised dramas furnish one means of bringing personal experiences and literature into the classroom. Dramatic improvisation allows students to create and act out situations from life and thus aids in personal growth by helping them to release tension, lose self-consciousness and gain self-awareness. Because it places the student in a human situation with other people, it calls for fairly quick thinking. Hence, it heightens one's perception and trains him to think and to express his thoughts in a clear, concise, and orderly way. Further, the creation of realistic dramas enables students to interact in much the same way that they will have to speak, think, write, and read in the outside world. It thus presents opportunities for exploring and understanding larger cultural and social relationships. A good way to introduce and to generate interest in a novel, short story, or a play is to present groups of students with critical situations from the work for dramatization. To insure spontaneity of response, ask students to read only to a point preceding the scene to be dramatized. Thus participants will not be aware of outcomes and behavior beforehand. The actors' only cue to action may be their knowledge of the situation, the other roles, and the behavior during the actual dramatization; or, to increase the lifelike quality of the situation, main persons in the cast may be given a bit of information about their attitudes, behavior, and background not shared by the other actors or the audience. The scenes may be recast with different students and acted out two or three times to acquire different responses to a situation. If desirable, a few minutes may be alloted for planning. Discussions after such dramatic presentations may lead to various kinds of writing activities—

stories, poems, personal letters, plays, and so forth. In such writing, students should choose their own subjects and, in many instances, their own forms.

Audiovisual media—cartoons, records, film and filmstrips, tapes, photographs, theater and movie trips—should be used to bring experiences into the classroom, for making literature live, and for generating discussion. Playing recordings of poems, plays, and stories while students follow in the text gives real voices to the words on the page and enables students to hear meanings and emotions, pronunciations and intonation patterns of both colloquial and literary language.

Contemporary essays and taped interviews provide effective means for bringing current issues into the life of the classroom. In addition to the teacher's selections, students should be allowed to bring to class essays on issues that interest them from current periodicals or recent collections. These may be read to the class as a whole, or small groups with similar interests may engage in discussions of the pros and cons concerning their topics. Informal debates may be organized for the benefit of the class as a whole. The teacher may also prepare taped interviews on a relevant issue. With the present popularity and convenience of the cassette tape recorder, such interviews can easily be planned, conducted, and recorded with public officials, drug addicts, police officers, prisoners, students, ministers, teachers, college administrators, and active members of civic and professional groups who are willing to air their social and political views. Recordings may also be made of poets reading their poems, or of artists, popular singers and musicians willing to comment on situations of current interest in society. These interviews may be structured and organized by the teacher's providing introductory comments and explanations to mark divisions and transitions in the progression of the tape. In like manner, students may make their own interviews or dictate their own views and opinions that can later be written in appropriate form. This kind of activity brings the issue to life in the classroom and enables the student to gain insights into others' views and learn to respect others' opinions while he formulates judgments which may be contrary to theirs. This activity also serves as a stimulus for writing, for it gives the student a variety of material to work with in organizing his thoughts. When students write, the teacher must encourage them to express their own individual and critical opinions in acceptable prose, without allowing form to outweigh interest or individuality. Meaningful discussion, therefore, should precede all writing assignments. This enables students to formulate their own views and decisions when they write instead of accepting those already imposed by society. Students should also be encouraged to spend time organizing and developing their rebuttals and comparisons, to provide suitable substantiation for their points, to draw from their own personal experiences as evidence for their contentions.

Although the teacher should not insist on standard English during initial attempts at writing and speaking, he must not allow critical language problems to be ignored and should later bring in more restrictions on correctness. He must make students aware that the outer world demands a certain command of standard language skills for acceptance. Thus, the teacher should encourage students to recognize the differences between their mode of speech—the speech required for living and interacting in the black community—and the mode of speech necessary for employment and advancement. He must not decry one, but help students to know and acknowledge the other. This can be done by correlating deviances in the black dialect with the standard form and letting students decide when and where standard expressions should be used. In addition to the students' own writing, poems written in dialect and short stories containing dialogues in dialect have proven effective in showing the contrast between the dialect and standard English, and for instilling respect for and recognition of dialect. Paul Laurence Dunbar's poems and Charles W. Chesnutt's folktales have worked well for this purpose. Students may be asked to read the poems and stories in groups, and each group may rewrite the poem or certain sections of the story in standard English. If students are presented with two poems by the same author, one in dialect and one in standard English, and asked to transcribe the dialect to standard English and vice versa noting the difference in tone and mood, this may emphasize the contrast and force an awareness that standard English is more appropriate for some purposes and modes of expression.

Evidence from research indicates that constant dwelling on grammar and rules has little effect on writing skills. The writing workshop approach provides one alternative to this method. Lessons on grammar and principles of writing may be conducted in this manner. These lessons should grow directly out of the students' writing and answer their immediate and individual needs. For this technique to be effective, however, the teacher must have a thorough knowledge of rules of grammar, rhetoric, and correct usage. Through the writing workshop approach, students can write for the class group rather than for the teacher, and the themes should be read and discussed in small groups. Students may exchange papers within the group, read them, write comments on them, and discuss them. The teacher circulates among the groups noting problems not raised. Later, after reviewing the students' papers and making his own comments and corrections, he projects or dittos pieces of writing and leads a discussion designed to elicit suggestions for revisions from the students. Note that corrections and revisions come mainly from the students with guidance and direction from the teacher. Establishing a writing center conducted by tutors and some teachers provides an excellent supportive service beyond the classroom. Individual conferences or tutorial sessions may also be set up for students experiencing serious difficulties in writing or in language usage.

Surely, for many obvious reasons, a student-centered, experience-centered curriculum will best serve the needs of black students. It allows for more human and personal interaction between teachers and students, more student involvement in the life of the classroom, greater concern for the integrity of the students' interests and experiences, and more emphasis on the students' personal growth and development —on discovering their identities and developing their skills and talents along the lines of significant interest to them. Thus, in addition to teaching communication skills, the teacher can aid the students in building confidence and in creating healthy self-images. The students can come to see that their ideas and experiences are significant and that they actually can do work that is good and important. They can also come to feel that the classroom may, potentially, allow them to work out for themselves the questions of who they are and where they're going in a complex world that offers them little direction. This kind of curriculum also provides for continued experimentation with materials and methods to find the most effective means of placing students in the context of experience, keeping them immersed in language and ideas, and enabling them to use, to handle language. Clearly such a curriculum places a burden of responsibility on the teacher. Thus, to be truly effective, the teacher must be educated to this approach. In-service workshops should therefore be set up on college campuses for planning, organizing, and designing curriculum materials and for instructing teachers in innovative approaches. Consultants should be brought in to acquaint teachers with techniques of dramatic improvisation, group dynamics, and other instructional practices.

A brief look at changes envisioned in English teaching

based on research done in the field along with a glimpse at the present status of English teaching in American colleges and universities will support our recommended change from the traditional method to the student-centered classroom approach to English instruction.

John Dixon's *Growth Through English* and James Moffett's *Teaching the Universe of Discourse* propose new directions in English teaching that react to the traditional notion of dissecting English into language, composition, and literature and teaching it as if it were a content course like history or science. Both Moffett and Dixon seek to define English by process rather than by content and attempt to describe the activities we engage in through language. They advocate a unitary rather than a fragmentary approach to English instruction, an approach that relates man's language to his experience, that uses language to handle, order, and come to terms with experience. One significant point that emerges from these authors is the concept of English as consisting principally of experience and involvement. Both Dixon and Moffett view the English classroom as a place where students come together to share experiences, as a place for interaction, as a place for the operational use of language to gain insight into the world at large and to serve individual growth and development. Clearly, then, they advocate a break with the constrictions of convention and a new emphasis on experience and on learning by internalizing skills in the process of using them in some purposeful activity. They believe that talk and drama in the classroom initiate this process of internalization, and it is further developed and extended through reading and writing.

The Basic Issues Conference, a cooperative effort between MLA and NCTE, marked the starting point for innovations in the English-teaching climate of the late 1950's and with the development of Curriculum Study Centers in the 1960's, interest broadened. In 1966 representatives from Britain,

Canada, and the United States met on the Dartmouth campus to compare practices and problems in English teaching. Dixon's *Growth Through English,* reporting the conclusions of this conference, was published in 1967 and Moffett's *Teaching the Universe of Discourse* was published in 1968. However, methods of teaching English in the freshman course in most American colleges and universities have, in large measure, remained unaffected.

An examination of articles on teaching freshman English in *College English* and *College Composition and Communication,* 1965–1972, reveals that although some attempts have been made at employing new approaches and techniques, basically, the teaching of freshman English has not changed or become more effective in the past few years. Generally, however, the movement is away from the traditional approach. Many authors criticize the traditional approach as detrimental and seek to find more suitable methods of teaching the freshman course. Most of the authors agree that the freshman course as it exists must be either revitalized or discarded completely. Thus, some colleges, for lack of a more desirable alternative, are abandoning freshman English altogether; many are reducing the amount of English that freshmen are required to take, while others are converting freshman English to a course in literature.

In an attempt to discover what methods are being used in predominantly black colleges, we sent questionnaires to forty of these schools in different sections of the country. Fourteen colleges responded to these questionnaires. In ten out of the fourteen schools, the freshman course is a combination of literature and composition. To a very limited degree, innovations have been introduced and audiovisual materials have become popular stimuli for student writing. All of the schools use works by black writers, but as one teacher wrote, "We stay away from controversial writers like Eldridge Cleaver." None of the schools use works by black writers alone, but include these along with other writers. This survey, of course, represents too small a sample to allow for general assumptions about teaching freshman English in the black colleges as a whole. However, as products of these schools, and as teachers of freshman English in them for a number of years, we feel confident in saying that except for those involved in some aspect of experimentation and innovation, and a few possible exceptions, freshman English courses in most black colleges are still basically caught up in the traditional methods.

One instance of educators making a concerted and successful effort to break with tradition and put into practice more viable teaching approaches is the Thirteen College Curriculum Program, founded by the Institute for Services to Education in 1967 and involving a consortium of black colleges. Located on each college campus is a kind of college within a college consisting of ten teachers, a director, a counselor, one hundred freshman, and one hundred sophomores. The goal of this program is to create an education based on the learner as doer by designing curricula structured around authentic experience.

The freshman English course, called "Ideas and Their Expression," combines composition and literature. Writing, however, is not taught simply as the production of clear expository prose, but as a part of the students' own search for identity and competence. The literature embodies a selection of paperbacks that changes from year to year and includes classics, contemporary writings, and works on popular and folk culture. The course uses works by black writers as a regular part of the curriculum, not as a separate unit on black studies. The course also makes extensive use of audiovisual materials, again mixing forms by both blacks and whites. Instead of chronology or periods as a principle of organization, the course is organized around certain themes—"Love," "Responsibility," "Alienation." One purpose of the juxtaposition of literature and other media is to create an environment in which students begin to find their own way—find new things to interest them, develop and exercise judgments, improve their ability to read and write, and find their own voices. In a student-centered classroom, students question authority and by doing so come to rely upon themselves as having valid opinions. Thus they see that their own experiences are meaningful and their relation to the world is clearer. Each summer, eight-week workshops are conducted for teacher orientation to new techniques, methods, and materials, and for teacher involvement in curriculum planning and revision.*

It should be noted, however, that colleges involved in this program reach only a small number of students, and the program as instituted on each campus involves only a part of the freshman class. It should also be noted that black colleges still enroll the greater portion of those black students who enter college. What are their freshman English courses doing for the rest of these black students? Surely, if they would take some cues from Moffett and Dixon, if they would make an effort to follow the example of the Thirteen College Curriculum Program, and if they would institute into their programs some of the recommended changes included in this paper, the freshman course would more effectively facilitate the personal and academic success of black students. The black college, say many black educators, should be experimental. Because of its very nature, the freshman English course lends itself to experimentation. Our appeal to freshman English faculties is to move away from tradition, be imaginative and creative, and experiment!

_____

* Information about the Thirteen College Curriculum Program may be found in Joseph Turner's *Making New Schools: The Liberation of Learning* (New York, 1971), pp. 145–161.

4

The Role of Black Studies in Music Education: A Critical Analysis

by Ellsworth Janifer

At the time of his untimely death on April 29, 1972, Dr. Ellsworth Janifer was professor of music and chairman of the Music and Art Department of Manhattan Community College of the City University of New York. He was a graduate of Howard University, the University of Michigan and the University of London where he received his Ph.D. in 1959.

The author of several articles on black music and musicians, he was coauthor, with Dr. Leonard Goines, of The Black Musical Experience *which is to be published in 1973 by Harper & Row.*

From the late years of the nineteenth century, music education in America has been dominated by a cultural bias derived from the assumption of white educators that Western European music is superior to any other in the world and therefore the only music worthy of serious study in the curriculum at all levels of the educational process. As a result, the music of black men the world over has been consistently and systematically excluded from the American educational process, and American children, both black and white, have been taught that African music—indeed anything African—is savage, primitive, and pagan, and that Afro-American music—blues, gospel music, rhythm and blues, and jazz—lacks

150

the sublimity, objectivity, logic, morality, and craftsmanship of Western art music.

This long, dreary record of obscurantist reaction that has been foisted upon black music by white educators, scholars, critics, and musicians has been the cause of incalculable damage to the pride, identity, self-esteem, and motivation for learning of black students. For generations, black people have received through both direct and indirect means, a crushing sense of cultural worthlessness and nothingness from their exposure to traditional American education. Indirectly, these feelings have been nurtured by the insidious omission of black achievements in all areas of human endeavor from the textbooks black children read. Even the most naïve schoolboy knows that only a people who have achieved anything worth recording are included in his textbooks. Blacks have traditionally been omitted; therefore, in his estimation, they have achieved nothing. As is well known, books, in the estimation of school children (and many adults), are infallible and do not lie.

Thus, at a time when black people are becoming increasingly more aware of their cultural heritage; at a time when black people have reclaimed their pride in blackness and have come to terms with their identity as an African people after centuries of shame and ambivalence toward their roots, few of them are aware, as Leonard Goines points out, that

> From the days of the white minstrels to the present day rock musicians, white artists and business men have assimilated and incorporated Black elements into their musical offerings. All of today's popular music, in fact, is based on various blends of blues and gospel forms.

Even more significantly, few educated blacks know anything about the great but unjustly obscured black jazz innovators such as Bunk Johnson, Fletcher Henderson, Don Redman, Joe "King" Oliver, Jelly Roll Morton, Sidney Bechet, James

P. Johnson, Clifford Brown, or Bud Powell. Fewer still know the troubled and turbulent stories of the great blues pioneers: W. C. Handy, Gertrude "Ma" Rainey, Blind Lemon Jefferson, Huddie Ledbetter, or Bessie Smith, and even smaller numbers are aware of the monumental role that the music of Africa and the Caribbean plays in their own musical heritage.

If the "lost" musical heritage of black Americans is to be reclaimed and made to be a meaningful, relevant force in their lives, an intensive program of re-education must be launched in which all the lies, myths, distortions, and propaganda of the past will be exposed and revealed for what they are. The only way that this can be done effectively is to revise completely existing curricula in music education for black students so that they will focus around the black musical experience, for as Terry François points out, "The first responsibility of any individual is to find out *who* he is, and then accept himself for *what* he is."

Although this can best be accomplished in predominantly black schools, predominantly white institutions must also provide black students with the same variety of courses in the black musical experience that they have so generously made available to white students for the study of Western European art music through the years. It should also be pointed out that such a curriculum will have equal relevance for white students as well, since they too have been victimized by the long-standing myths and propaganda about black music. Furthermore, black-oriented music courses can be effective agents for change by assisting white students in gaining valuable insight into the extent that racism has perverted the lives of black Americans, and how they, as members of the white majority, can be helpful in eradicating this cancerous virus from American society.

The idea that the black experience should be the focal point of education for black students in all areas of the curriculum is certainly not original with this essay. The Hampton Intermediate School in Detroit, for instance, has developed a curriculum in which "black pride is taught as thoroughly as mathematics or music and has become an integral part of subjects and activities." Similarly, at Howard University, an institution whose curriculum in music, until recently, has been completely devoted to Western European art music, a subcommittee of faculty and students entrusted with the task of developing criteria for the selection of a new Dean of the College of Fine Arts recently created a furor by subscribing to the theory that education in music should be centered around the black experience:

> The objective of increased emphasis upon black awareness, the black experience, and the black perspective can best be implemented in the College of Fine Arts by revising completely existing curricula so that the courses of instruction are centered about the black experience with supplemental instruction in Euro-American culture.

At Manhattan Community College (the City University of New York), the Department of Music and Art now offers a new curriculum in music with two major options: Western European art music and jazz performance. The major in jazz, including such courses as Jazz History, Music in World Culture, Jazz Theory, Jazz Performance, and Improvisation, provides black students with the option of concentrating their musical studies in the black experience if they so desire.

Nevertheless, as Professor Goines observes, some music educators, both black and white, will misinterpret or "conveniently misunderstand" the idea that the black musical experience should be the focal point of music courses for black students because of its long history of neglect and abuse at the hands of the educational Establishment. Other music educators will undoubtedly argue that stressing the black experience in music is reverse racism. However, as Professor

Goines further maintains, "This is a silly outlook and an offensive one. It can no more be viewed as racism for a black student to trace the history and development of black music from its African beginnings than it is for his white counterpart to trace the history and development of white Western music from its European beginnings."

If, then, in these black-oriented music courses, our approach is "meaningful, relevant, and educationally sound" and results in "setting the record straight" and "telling the truth," most students "black and white, in college, secondary, or elementary schools will benefit from them." But even more significantly, it is important for all educators to give considerable thought to Miller's splendid conclusion: "Far from restricting black students to the study of their culture alone . . . the major motivation of black studies is to entice students who were previously conditioned to exclusion to greater involvement in the educational process." Nowhere can this be done with greater effectiveness than in music, the most creative, the most expressive, the most demanding, and the most crucial of all the black cultural arts.

At the present time, the trend in most American high schools and colleges is to accept the token approach to the teaching of black music by incorporating it into existing courses, such as music appreciation and general music. The pitfalls and dangers of this approach are clearly illustrated in the *Music Appreciation Curriculum Bulletin for New York City High Schools,* Curriculum Bulletin No. 4, 1969–1970 series, hereafter cited as the "New York City syllabus."

In spite of the fact that the ethnic ratio in New York City schools varies from 96 percent to 2 percent black, and in some schools, more than half the students are Puerto Rican, the high school curriculum in music appreciation was designed by a curriculum committee of twelve educators, all white and all chairmen of music departments in academic high schools. Even the evaluative judgment for the curriculum was provided by two white professors: Jerrold Ross, chairman, Music Department, New York University School of Music Education, and Paul Glass, professor of music, Brooklyn College. Apparently, the committee did not see fit to include a music chairman from a vocational high school (where most black students are enrolled) or a black music educator as a member of the committee or as a consultant. Moreover, when the curriculum was tried out in various high schools, such predominantly black high schools as Haaren, Boys High, Benjamin Franklin, Brandeis, and Charles Evans Hughes were not invited to participate. This raises a serious question of fundamental importance: For whom was this curriculum really structured in the first place?

A thorough study of the syllabus will reveal that the curriculum committee feels beyond the slightest doubt that Western European art music is unquestionably good while black music—particularly blues, gospel music, and rhythm and blues—is unquestionably bad. Thus, at the outset, the stage is set for a dramatic cultural confrontation between the black student and the white teacher, for it certainly is no secret that all of the music chairmen and most of the music teachers in the New York City high schools are white.

The only possible answer to our question then, under the circumstances, is that the New York City syllabus was basically designed for white middle-class students. For while the syllabus pays the merest lip service to black American music, and to a much lesser extent the music of Africa and Asia, it practically ignores the cultural heritage of Puerto Rico and the Caribbean. There is no question, then, that black and Puerto Rican students will see it for exactly what it is—a glorification of white Western culture, and just another "put-down" of the black and Puerto Rican cultural heritage. Closer inspection of the contents of some of the study units of the syllabus will confirm this point of view.

The introduction clearly points out that class singing should constitute one of the major activities in high school music classes. A basic list of about 190 songs is given, including patriotic and service songs, national heritage songs, American folk songs and ballads, spirituals, songs and ballads from other lands, songs of brotherhood, songs for community singing, standard popular songs, songs from operettas and musicals, seasonal songs, sacred songs, art songs, game songs, and sentimental songs. With the exception of the spirituals, which are now museum pieces, highly respected but rarely performed in black churches or communities, few of these songs are relevant to the urban black experience. And some, because of their racist associations, are highly objectionable. Such songs as "In the Evening by the Moonlight You Can Hear Those Darkies Singing," a white minstrel song, and "Marching to Pretoria," a white South African (Afrikaans) folk song, are particularly offensive to black people. As a matter of fact, in the category of songs entitled "Songs and Ballads from Other Lands," Italian, Irish, English, Welsh, and Scottish songs predominate while the great and varied wealth of songs from black America, Africa, and the Caribbean is practically ignored. Quite predictably, this will leave black and Caribbean students with the false notion that their musical heritage is inferior to that of Western Europe.

While several of these songs glorify the beauty of white womanhood—"Beautiful Dreamer," "Jeanie With the Light Brown Hair," "Annie Laurie"—there are absolutely none which even mention black femininity in any capacity at all, despite the fact that such songs do exist, especially in the vast and varied repertory of the blues. Harry T. Burleigh's sensitive and delicate setting of Langston Hughes' "Lovely Dark and Lonely One" is also a good example which might well have been used.

In preparing a list of basic songs for urban black students in 1969–70 it is also well to keep in mind that sentimental songs expressive of nineteenth century white middle-class tastes, cloying operetta tunes from the 1890's, service songs which glorify war and conquest, songs by Stephen Foster which romanticize slavery, pompously inflated American patriotic songs, and antebellum spirituals are simply not sung by black youngsters anymore.

As painful as it may be for some educators to accept, gospel music, rhythm and blues, and jazz are the preferred music of the ghetto. In a very real sense, rhythm and blues interprets life in the urban inner city in idiomatic musical language and trenchant verbal allusions which black youngsters understand and thoroughly relate to. It is important to bear in mind that such rhythm-and-blues hits as "Say It Loud, I'm Black and I'm Proud," "Power to the People," "Get Involved!" and "We're Gonna' Make It," echo positive political and social goals of the black community. It is also well to remember that like black athletes, rhythm-and-blues stars are among the most respected figures in the black community. Black youngsters avidly collect their recordings, follow their itineraries, emulate their dress, and imitate their vocal idioms with amazing fidelity. It therefore stands to reason that any musical curriculum designed for urban black students that does not realize the tremendous significance of rhythm and blues in their lives is literally asking for failure.

Another troublesome area of this syllabus is Unit 11, entitled "Music in America: A Survey of Our Heritage." This unit all but dismisses Afro-American music as a viable study unit by throwing it together with diverse musical types which have little or no relevance to it, such as Irish-Scotch reels and jigs, English ballads, minstrel songs, popular songs from musicals, songs from movies, the band movement, and serious music. As a result, Afro-American music, which really should be treated as a separate unit because of its unfamiliarity to black students and because of its long history of exclusion and denigration, is fragmented and diluted, and ultimately reduced to a place of peripheral significance. To make matters worse, the authors state in no uncertain terms that they regard "serious music" to be of greater value than jazz or folk music:

> In any case, neither folk music nor jazz should be allowed to dominate the unit to the exclusion of serious composition. Since most music written in the lighter vein has only transient importance, the status of serious music as still representing the best hope for immortality should be upheld and even promoted.

Regardless of what the authors think of the aesthetic and academic value of jazz, they cannot deny the fact that it is the greatest phenomenon of American music in the twentieth century. Yet, aside from the vague statement of intent to "trace the evolution of modern jazz through the spiritual, blues, ragtime, and Dixieland," and the inclusion of a chart tracing the historical course of Afro-American music, there is little else of significance said about it in the entire syllabus although extensive coverage is given to the works of so-called "serious composers" such as Copland, Menotti, Ives, and Barber.

By not so subtle indirection, the authors of the syllabus give the erroneous impression that the contributions of blacks to American music have been limited exclusively to jazz and spirituals. Yet, from the statements made concerning the origins of the spirituals in another unit (African Music, Unit 15), there seems to be some ambiguity in their minds as to whether or not the spirituals are, in fact, the original creations of black Americans:

> For fifty years slaves had been singing the old hymns and psalm tunes; however, through the process of Africanization and the lack of musical notation, both words and music were so altered as to scarcely resemble the prototype.

The "white-to-black" theory of the origins of Afro-American spirituals found fertile soil during the 1920's and 1930's in the writings of three white Southerners: Newman White, George Pullen Jackson, and Guy B. Johnson. Their basic contention was that whatever African elements may be present in Afro-American spirituals—and they did not study African music to any significant degree—the correspondence between them and the white camp-meeting hymns of the Southern highlands are so close and numerous that one need search no further for the origins of the former. The supporting evidence for these extravagant claims was largely confined to studies of Afro-American spirituals as they related to white religious music.

A comparison of the following passage from George Pullen Jackson's "Genesis of the Negro Spiritual" (*American Mercury*, June, 1932) with the statement quoted from the New York City syllabus will reveal definite similarities in concept:

> I have not yet gone as far as I hope to into my study of the parent songs in comparison with their Negro offspring. But my findings thus far justify the assertion that the former show most of the ear-marks observable in the latter . . . To be sure, the Negro seems to have loosened up the white man's metrical patterns, limbered up his harmony, determined pitch intervals, and injected a wealth of emotion which was not there before. But who can prove that he really did so?

It is instructive to point out here that the "white-to-black" theory of the origins of Afro-American spirituals was effectively challenged in the works of such black scholars as W. E. Burghardt Du Bois, John Wesley Work, Sr., and James Weldon Johnson. But it was Melville Herskovits, in his definitive work *The Myth of the Negro Past* (New York: Harper, 1942) who applied the final *coup de grâce* to the racist speculations of White, Jackson, and Guy B. Johnson by exposing the unscientific nature and the inconclusiveness of their research, and by proving (with the assistance of Kolinski, Herzog, and

Hornbostel) that African retentions in the spirituals were the most fundamental influence in their development.

Despite the availability of Herskovits' work, however, the authors of the New York City syllabus continue to expound the "white-to-black" theory and even include George Pullen Jackson's *White and Negro Spirituals* (New York: J. J. Augustin, 1944) in their list of teacher references.

Finally, as if to document their contention that the major contributions of blacks to American music have been limited exclusively to spirituals and jazz, the authors of the New York City syllabus proceeded to omit black composers entirely from the section of the unit on "Music in America" entitled "Compositions in Classical Forms." It is difficult to understand how the committee could have omitted William Grant Still (the dean of black American composers) and Ulysses Kay, two of the most distinguished black composers of music in Western art forms. It is even more unfortunate that they saw fit to eliminate the younger generation of contemporary black composers—George Walker, Stephen Chambers, Arthur Cunningham, Hale Smith, Olly Wilson—whose work, as Howard Klein, a *New York Times* music critic, points out, "strikes one forcibly upon first hearing that these are not the doctrinaire composers we have gotten used to . . . Their music has life, it pulsates with human energies and reminds us that music can communicate and still be modern."

Significantly, it is Black Studies programs in music rather than music appreciation textbooks or histories of music that have given these composers a good deal of the recognition they so richly deserve. Is it too much to ask that a school system with one of the largest enrollments of black students in this country should broaden its rather narrow horizons and let these students know that black men too are composers of Western art music?

Turning our attention now to Unit 4 ("Music of the Theater"), we find that once again music of black composers is omitted, further reinforcing the impression that black composers have contributed nothing in the areas of the Broadway musical, the ballet, films, opera, and operetta.

Nothing could be further from the truth. Traditionally, the theater has been one of the richest and most exciting vehicles for black musicians and actors. From the great traditional rituals of West Africa to the mimetic singing and dancing of the antebellum plantation in which the sadistic slavemaster forced the slave to caricature himself; from the nineteenth-century minstrel and medicine shows to the twentieth century all-black Broadway musicals and vaudeville acts; from the great operatic scores of Clarence Cameron White and William Grant Still in the thirties and forties to the dynamic contemporary black theater with incidental music, black histrionic and musical genius have collaborated in inimitable theatrical splendor.

Regardless of this glorious tradition, however, the only theatrical music even remotely related to the black experience in this unit is a vague reference to *Carmen Jones* and to Gershwin's *Porgy and Bess,* both of which are particularly offensive to most black people.

The tendency to magnify the importance of Gershwin with reference to black music as evidenced by *Porgy and Bess* is not unique with the New York City syllabus. In syllabus after syllabus, in textbook after textbook, one constantly comes across references to Gershwin's "sympathetic" and "original" treatment of jazz and black folk music. The authors of the New York City syllabus allege, for example, that Gershwin's absorption of African elements in *Porgy and Bess* rivals those found in spirituals and other black folk music! These are indeed inflated claims for *Porgy and Bess* and they call for a closer, more critical look at Gershwin and his association with black folk music.

Porgy and Bess, subtitled an "American Folk Opera," with its garish fusion of imitation black folk music, Broadway hit tunes, and Italian and Russian grand opera, has no relevance whatsoever to the *real* black experience in America. No one knew this any better than Sidney Bechet, a seminal figure in the history of New Orleans jazz and one of the greatest black musicians of all times:

> What's Negro music? . . . I suppose most people would think right away of that show *Porgy and Bess.* But what do you call a thing like that—symphonic jazz? That's not real Jazz. There's some feeling there, it's a nice show; but that's about the closest it comes. There's one or two nice pieces to it: *Summertime,* that's one that's nice, in that you get just about the closest to the mood of Negro music. But listen to it, listen to it real careful—you get a feeling of *St. Louis Blues* there. It's a borrowed feeling . . . But it still isn't Negro music. It still isn't saying what the black man, he'd say.

In its stereotyped portrayal of South Carolina blacks as lazy, promiscuous, violent, banjo-strumming niggers to the utter delight of the affluent white theatergoing set of the depression-ridden 1930's, it is, as Harold Cruse astutely observes, a "product of American developments that were intended to shunt Negroes off into a tight box of sub-cultural artistic dependence, stunted growth, caricature, aesthetic self-mimicry imposed by others, and creative insolvency." Viewed in this sense, it is indeed a white American folk opera, for as Cruse further relates, black people "had no part in writing, producing, or staging it" and when the first "authorized" recordings were made by Victor Records (under the personal supervision of Gershwin) shortly after the opening, white singers—Lawrence Tibbett and Helen Jepson—were engaged to perform the principal roles. The black artists—Todd Duncan and Ann Brown—who created the roles on Broadway were simply not permitted to reap the financial benefits of a historic "first" recording.

But let us look at *Porgy and Bess* from a black point of

view. What a stroke of real genius it would have been if Gershwin could have had the critical insight and genuine sympathy for his characters to exploit Porgy's crippled condition as a symbol of the perverse castration of the black man by a racist-oriented society: a man crippled and rendered impotent by the heavy oppressive weight of a society in which the legal, economic, and educational systems formed a conspiracy to subvert his manhood, destroy his humanity, steal and exploit his culture, and reduce him to a social, cultural, and economic nonentity. Of course, as every black man in America knows full well, the Porgy of the *real* black experience laughs, drinks, and dances in what little leisure time he enjoys to blot out the horrible specter of racism and exploitation which he must of necessity face during his working hours. In short, as black folk poets put it, he "laughs to keep from crying." His hostility toward himself and toward his own people (which both Gershwin and his librettist DuBose Heyward portray as an ethnic trait!) stems from his suppressed anger at the system that denies his manhood, yet forbids him to strike back; that reviles his culture while it grows fat and sleek from copying it; that laughs at him in a phony folk opera about black people while it would categorically reject the truth about the real black experience in a comparable work written by a black man. Thus, the derivative minstrel song, "I Got Plenty o' Nuthin'" which assumes a central position in the opera as Porgy's credo, is an insult to every black man in America. No black man, no matter how beaten and bruised, no matter how depraved, no matter how happy-go-lucky, would ever give vent to his deep personal grief and frustration by singing a minstrel song reveling in his own castration at the hands of his racist oppressor. If Porgy is to be believed, he would sing a super black blues in the finest tradition of Leadbelly, Son House, Bukka White, or Robert Johnson, all of whom were alive but conveniently "invisible" to Gershwin when he was composing his opera.

In spite of the fact that Gershwin is said to have visited South Carolina to observe black people and to have taken part in their singing and shouting at revivals in order to get the "feel" of their music, *Porgy and Bess* is nothing more than the fantasy of a rich white Broadway tunesmith who had absorbed, no matter how unconsciously, all the racist propaganda about blacks so typical of white Americans during the 1930's. To equate *Porgy and Bess* with African music or black American folk music, as the New York City syllabus attempts to do, vitiates the very concept of both. As Harold Cruse so rightly maintains,

> *Porgy and Bess* should be forever banned by all Negro performers in the United States. No Negro singers, actors, or performers should ever submit to a role in this vehicle again. If white producers want to stage this folk-opera it should be performed by white performers in blackface, because it is distorted imitation all the way through.

If *Porgy and Bess* is used in music appreciation classes designed for black students, it should be exposed for what it is rather than paraded as a classic of the American musical theater. To do otherwise is to lie to black students. To link it with black American folk music as an example of the influence of African music on American music is such a monstrous perversion of the truth that it literally staggers the imagination and exposes in stark relief the authors' total ignorance of both African and Afro-American music.

The authors' ignorance of the contributions of black composers to the American musical theater is no less appalling and could have been alleviated with a small amount of modest research.

No discussion of the American musical theater is complete without some reference to *Shuffle Along* (1921) by Eubie Blake and Noble Sissle, which spearheaded the trend toward all-black Broadway musicals between 1921 and 1930 and which is "one of the outstanding musicals of that or any day." As a matter of fact, several of Blake's tunes from *Shuffle Along*—"I'm Just Wild About Harry," "Love Will Find a Way," "Bandanna Days," and "Gypsy Blues"—became national hits. Fats Waller's *Hot Chocolates* (1929) (from which the inimitable "Ain't Misbehavin' " comes) is also worthy of consideration as are selected works by Will Marion Cook (*Clorindy—The Origin of the Cakewalk,* 1898) and James Rosamond Johnson (*The Red Moon,* 1908), two more prolific black composers of musical shows.

Scott Joplin, the fabulous "King of Ragtime," one of the finest albeit one of the most unjustly neglected of black American composers, was strongly attracted to the theater although his work in this genre is completely overshadowed by his magnificent piano rags which have recently been rediscovered by critics and musicologists. Although the musical score to Joplin's first opera—*A Guest of Honor*—has been lost, *Treemonisha,* his second and most representative opera, is full of beautiful, finely constructed music, equal in every respect to his justly famed piano rags. It should occupy a prominent place in the unit under discussion, especially since it is far more relevant to the black experience than *Porgy and Bess* could ever hope to be.

Two black composers have distinguished themselves in the field of grand opera. William Grant Still's four operas—*Troubled Island* (1938), *A Bayou Legend* (1940), *Blue Steel* (1935), and *A Southern Legend* (1942)—though still in manuscript certainly deserve recognition and study. Clarence Cameron White's towering *Ouanga* (1931), an expansive musical portrait of Dessalines, Haiti's great liberator and defender, is a brilliant and exciting work and should have special appeal for Caribbean students.

While the film industry has been notable for its exclusion of blacks from practically all areas except in the most menial and condescending capacities, black composers have produced film scores that compare favorably with those by white composers mentioned in the New York City syllabus. Among these are James P. Johnson's *Yamaceraw* (*c.* 1930), a film score for a short on Bessie Smith, Quincy Jones's scores for *The Pawnbroker, Mirage, The Slender Thread,* and *Walk Don't Run,* Herbie Hancock's music for *Blowup,* Booker T. Jones's (of Booker T. and the MG's) score for the Jules Dassin film *Up Tight,* and Ulysses Kay's lovely score for *The Quiet One.* It is almost certain that most black students are hardly aware of the existence of any film music by black composers. Considering their virtual addiction to the cinema (largely as a vehicle of escape), discovery of this music would be a joyful revelation to them.

Finally, some mention should be made of the use of incidental music in the contemporary black theater. Quite often, music for these performances has strong ethnic appeal, usually African or West Indian. Derek Walcott's *Dream on Monkey Mountain,* recently presented by the Negro Ensemble Company of New York·City, has a splendid background of West Indian and African folk music and dances. Joseph Walker's *Ododo* is a powerful evocation of the music of traditional West African rituals, while Archie Shepp's music to LeRoi Jones's *Slave Ship* is so gripping and telling that it literally hypnotizes the audience.

Familiarity with the contributions of black musicians to the American musical theater can be a most fulfilling and satisfying experience for black students who have been deprived of knowledge about it for far too long. To continue to deprive them of the richness and breadth of much of this music while overexposing them to Victor Herbert, Jacques Offenbach, Gilbert and Sullivan, Rodgers and Hammerstein, and Franz Lehar is as unrealistic as it is reprehensible.

The unit on African music (Unit 15) had the potential for being one of the most exciting and relevant sections of the New York City syllabus. Aside from the widespread interest in African history, dress, hair styles, languages, arts, and dances that is now common among black Americans in general, many black youngsters of high school age are particularly inspired by the political concept of Pan-Africanism—the unification of all peoples of African descent in a worldwide political and cultural bond. Throughout black communities across the nation, the red, black, and green standard that symbolized the Garvey Movement in the 1920's has become synonymous with "Black Liberation," and the revived interest in Africa as the fatherland of all black people. Never before in history have black Americans so passionately and intensely devoted themselves to the pursuit of knowledge and learning about Africa, their ancestral home.

Therefore, a strong study unit on African music, particularly in predominantly black high schools, could not have failed to be overwhelmingly popular as well as dramatically successful from an educational point of view. It would have tied together all the diverse interests of black people in Africa, for music is inextricably interrelated with other aspects of African culture.

However, instead of dealing with African music as an integral part of African culture, the authors of the syllabus were merely content to trace what they considered to be African influences in antebellum spirituals and Gershwin's *Porgy and Bess*. For some strange reason, black secular music was omitted from their so-called comparative study.

This narrow and restricted approach to the study of African music resembles the rather circumscribed view fostered by the nineteenth-century German school of comparative or "primitive" musicology. Their interest in African music was limited to the collection of scientific data about the music in order to facilitate their search for parallels that might enhance their understanding of the origins of Western art music. The underlying philosophy of this school—"that the music of the most primitive peoples has preserved a very early stage of evolution without the interference of higher civilizations"—was codified in the writings of its philosophical leader, Curt Sachs.

By using a similar comparative approach, limited to the structural analysis of African music, the authors of the New York City syllabus also make it clear that they too are interested in African music only insofar as it can enhance their understanding of a minute segment of African-derived and Western art music. They apparently had no interest or knowledge of African music as a viable artistic entity in its own right. Professor J. H. Kwabena Nketia has warned of the dangers inherent in such a limited approach to the study of African music:

> Structural studies pursued in isolation without regard to other problems raised by the practice of the music are of course insufficient in African musical studies, for music is influenced not only by artistic considerations but also by social, religious, economic or practical considerations or by the requirements of the dance and other forms of artistic expression. Indeed one should attach more weight to such studies if one wishes to understand what African music means to those who make it or listen to it in social life.

One last word on this subject of African music. With the large number of black students enrolled in the New York City schools, and with the widespread interest in African culture which I have called attention to, it is difficult to understand why courses in the performance of African music have not been instituted in the music curriculum at all levels of instruction. Of all the ethnic groups that make up the population of New York City, black people are the only ones who cannot perform the music of their ancestral heritage. This, of course, has been due to the long years of black ambivalent and negative thought about Africa, and to the neglect and exclusion by white educators whose views of what is "good" and "musically desirable" apparently do not extend to African music any more than they do to Afro-American or Caribbean music.

There are other areas of the New York City syllabus that need critical rethinking; however, space limitations permit only a brief discussion of them here. The unit on "Types of Voices" (Unit 3), for example, laments "the growing admiration for careless vocalization in much rock-and-roll singing" and recommends that rock-and-roll "should be countered by demonstrations of highly trained [operatic] singing."

It is essential, however, that any music teacher of black students realize, as Stephen Henderson writes, that the so-called "careless vocalization" and by extension, the black-oriented vocal quality of rock-and-roll music, usually described by white critics as "reedy," "tinny," or "strident," is a "black cultural value" as old as Africa itself and deeply cherished by black people as a part of their cultural heritage. To ask black students from the ghetto to emulate the white operatic singing voice is tantamount to asking them to bleach their skins, straighten their hair, and to discard their natural speech patterns in order to adopt the cultural patterns of white America from whose values they have been alienated all their lives. Moreover, as black people know only too well, America has a dual standard when it comes to accepting or rejecting black speech patterns and the black singing voice. She takes what she wishes from both, ruthlessly exploits them—Janis Joplin, the Righteous Brothers, Tom Jones, and the Osmond Brothers are superb examples—and then self-righteously prattles about the problems of "culturally deprived" blacks whose "hard" and "raw" singing voices are so inappropriate for "serious" music, newscasting, opera, and the "legitimate" theater. Such calculated cultural hypocrisy only serves to alienate black students further.

Patriotic songs, school songs, and songs of the four armed services comprise a significant amount of the recommended song material for use in assembly and class singing in the New York City syllabus. Two of the most prominent aims of the unit on "Patriotic Songs" (Unit 1) are "to encourage a love and respect for patriotic and school songs" and "to give pupils an understanding of the nature of patriotic songs." Curiously, the authors apparently fail to realize that the *real* reason for teaching anyone patriotic songs is to foster "a love and respect" for one's country rather than for the country's national anthem. However, one way of achieving these goals (as stated) for black high school students, many of whom, as I have indicated, are already disillusioned with the American system, is to include in the unit material which fosters feelings of black pride and racial achievement, and which tends to reflect the self-image of black students in a strongly positive manner.

James Weldon Johnson's "Lift Every Voice and Sing," set to music by his brother, James Rosamond Johnson, would achieve these goals admirably. Yet the authors ignore it even though they recommend and encourage the study of European national anthems. Those of France, England, Israel, Germany, and Canada are specifically recommended.

Originally written in 1925 for black school children in Jacksonville, Florida, "Lift Every Voice and Sing" endows the black struggle with dignity and hope in a strongly positive way that few other songs have ever been able to equal. So great was its initial appeal to black Americans that it soon came to be nationally known as "The Negro National Anthem." It fell into obscurity during the years when the black middle-class struggle for integration dictated its supression as an undesirable symbol of black separatism and nationalism. With the recent surge of black awareness and identity, however, it has once again come into national prominence among black Americans. It is sung wherever black people congregate in large numbers, often to the exclusion of "The Star-Spangled Banner," and in predominantly black schools, students are demanding that it be given equal prominence with the national anthem in assembly programs and other school functions.

For its therapeutic value alone, "Lift Every Voice and Sing" should be included in any song repertory proposed for black students. But more than this, the song has positive historical and cultural significance to black people as one of the "first fruits" of the Harlem Renaissance, which together with the Garvey Movement was one of the most authentic black-oriented movements in the history of black Americans.

As may well be expected, the units on "Choral Music" and "The Art Song" (Units 5 and 6) continue the noted tendency to ignore the achievements of black composers. Several of the magnificent choral arrangements of Afro-American spirituals by Harry T. Burleigh, William Levi Dawson, Robert Nathaniel Dett, and John Wesley Work, Sr., are now permanent staples in the repertory of choral groups throughout the nation and are widely performed at choral concerts. Yet only one of these arrangements—Dett's "Listen to the Lambs"—is listed among the fifty or more short choral works recommended by the committee for performance by high school groups. Among the larger choral works by black composers, Samuel Coleridge-Taylor's "Hiawatha's Wedding Feast," Dett's "The Ordering of Moses" and "Chariot Jubilee," and William Grant Still's "And They Lynched Him on a Tree" are all handsome works and would provide a refreshingly different musical exposure for students of *any* ethnic background who are interested in singing fresh, unhackneyed choral literature.

Of all the forms of Western art music, black composers have particularly excelled in and have been most prolific in the composition of art songs. This is probably because it is easier for them to have songs published than elaborate symphonic works, and because there is an abundance of black concert singers to perform their songs. Having a large-scale work performed by a symphony orchestra still presents almost insurmountable difficulties to black composers. I do not think it is an exaggeration to point out that there is not one symphonic work by a black composer in the permanent repertory of any major symphony orchestra in this country. And, too, good phonograph recordings of their larger works are few and far between. This is the point behind the two recent record albums—*The Black Composer in America* (DC7107) and *Natalie Hinderas Plays Music by Black Composers* (DC7102/3)—devoted exclusively to the music of black composers: They are simply tired of being ignored by the musical Establishment.

Art songs, then, serve the purposes of black composers very well and some of them, particularly Burleigh, Coleridge-Taylor, Will Marion Cook, James Rosamond Johnson, and Margaret Bonds have spoken eloquently and poetically in this medium. But in spite of this, out of the 100 art songs listed in the syllabus, the committee apparently considered only one by a black composer—Howard Swanson's setting of Langston Hughes' *The Negro Speaks of Rivers*—to be worthy of mention!

The problem with the unit on the art song does not end here. A study unit on the art song intended for black students must of necessity include a discussion of Marian Anderson and Roland Hayes, two of the greatest lieder singers that America has produced, and a study of the solo arrangements of Afro-American spirituals by Harry T. Burleigh, Hall Johnson, and others—those authentic black art songs, born of suffering, sorrow, and indescribable pain.

Black students should especially know about Paul Robeson, that great black singer-actor and freedom fighter. His historic career began in New York in 1925 with a concert devoted solely to black spirituals which he felt were "the soul of the race made manifest." From this auspicious beginning (which marked the first all-black concert in history) he went on to bring the spiritual as an art form to a foremost position on the concert stages of the world.

In the history of black musical studies, Robeson is a seminal figure who anticipated the contemporary Black Studies movement by over forty years. The following excerpt from his article on black culture in 1934 may very well have been written by a black music student in 1971:

> Critics have often reproached me for not becoming an opera star and never attempting to give recitals of German and Italian songs as every singer is supposed to do. I am not an artist in the sense in which they want me to be an artist and of which they could approve. I have no desire to interpret the vocal genius of half a dozen cultures which are really alien to me. I have a far more important task to perform.
>
> When I first suggested singing Negro spirituals for English audiences, a few years ago, I was laughed at . . . And yet I have found response amongst this very audience to the simple, direct emotional appeal of Negro spirituals. These songs are to Negro culture what the works of the great poets are to English culture: they are the soul of the race made manifest.

Even in this brief discussion of black composers and performers of art songs, we see that a rich, untapped source of the black musical experience has been denied black students by a curriculum committee that is probably unaware of its existence and very likely unconvinced of its significance, and herein lies the problem. But let me hasten to add that this material is of the utmost significance to young black students thirsting for knowledge about their culture and heritage. If this relevant information cannot be included in traditionally oriented music appreciation courses, then it must be included in courses centered about the black musical experience. There is no viable alternative.

I have dealt at length with the New York City syllabus for

high schools because New York City with its teeming ghettos represents in microcosm the problems of all urban black communities in America today: de facto segregated schools coupled with massive pupil underachievement; the emergence of a hard core element within the black school population which is becoming more and more unresponsive to traditional educational patterns; drug-infested public schools; inadequate medical care; high unemployment among black youth; excessively high dropout rates; cultural isolation; and rodent-infested, substandard housing. If New York City with its vast and unprecedented wealth of human, material, and cultural resources cannot guarantee black students the educational tools to deal adequately with themselves as human beings and with the pathology of the ghetto which molds their lives, what is the answer for similarly besieged cities whose more limited resources render them even more helpless than New York City in solving the staggering problems of black Americans?

Against this background of massive urban decay and deterioration, the New York City syllabus with its rigid middle-class emphasis upon the cultural superiority of Western European art music, its ambivalent treatment of Afro-American music, its flagrant ignoring of the musical heritage of Africa and the Caribbean, and its insensitive inclusion of study materials offensive to black people is woefully inadequate for black high school students at the most crucial juncture of their lives.

Ironically, Harlem is the cultural center of black America, and the most progressive ideas of the new black cultural and political movements are beamed from there to the rest of the nation and thence to black people throughout the world. In view of this, it is unthinkable that twelve white music educators could produce a syllabus intended for the education of urban black children which utterly fails to take into consideration the cultural, social, and political changes that have been plainly evident in black communities throughout the country for the past ten years.

New York City, like every other city with comparable populations of blacks, needs a curriculum in music education centered around the black musical experience and developed by black music educators in consultation with cultural leaders in the black community. Traditional curricula in American music education have been developed for and by the affluent members of the white majority, and even after the post-World War II migrations of blacks to the cities virtually revolutionized urban education, music educators have shown little or no inclination toward sorely needed change in curriculum practices. Music appreciation courses continue to reflect the cultural values of the white majority, and the multi-ethnic nature of our society continues to be overlooked or ignored.

Therefore, a black-oriented curriculum in music is a necessary (but perhaps temporary) measure which is required to give music education in America the universality and objectivity it so badly needs. When white music educators accept the fact that America is a multi-ethnic society with diverse and contrasting cultural traditions, when they realize that if any ethnic group in the United States has its own viable culture, it is certainly the blacks, and when, as Professor Goines points out, they accept the fact that "all cultures—musical included—are complete under normal conditions" and that "one might differ from, but is equal to the other," then and only then will the need for a black-oriented music curriculum be rendered superfluous.

Black college students also face severe problems in studying the history and development of their musical heritage in meaningful and fulfilling academic settings. College students, however, are generally not as slavishly bound to the curriculum of academic departments as high school students are, and they have a freer choice in the selection of professors, which makes a good deal of difference. Besides, the recent demands of black college students for more relevant courses in the black experience in all academic disciplines have led to the institution of new courses in black music, although a traditional course in music appreciation (or music theory) is nonetheless frequently required as a prerequisite. Generally speaking, one-semester courses in black music have been instituted at the undergraduate level and are usually limited to instruction in Afro-American music or the history of jazz. Courses in African music, Latin and Caribbean music, world music, or such specialized areas of Afro-American music as the history of the blues are far less likely to be offered. Courses in rhythm and blues are practically nonexistent in most American colleges and universities, black or white. Rhythm and blues therefore remains the most "segregated" branch of black music.

Though the opportunities for black students to major in jazz performance are gradually increasing, these programs still encounter considerable resistance from faculties and administrations in most American institutions of higher learning. As a result, black students who are interested in jazz careers are often forced to pursue majors in art music even though there is little likelihood that the majority of them will find jobs in symphony orchestras, opera, musical comedy (except in all-black productions), television, and radio.

Indeed, in its December, 1970, issue, the *Bulletin of Negro History* found it necessary to speak out against the shameful exclusion of black instrumentalists from the major symphony orchestras:

> Several symphony orchestras have begun to use black musicians in their membership lists. Token appointments are: The Boston Symphony has a harpist and had a cellist; the New York Philharmonic Orchestra has a violinist; Cleveland Orchestra has a cellist; and Pittsburgh Symphony has a violinist. Two black musicians have joined

the Philadelphia Orchestra, a violinist and a violist . . . If you know of others, advise us. This is a field which should be *plied open* and most of us know of musicians who could apply and would make good. (Italics mine)

The situation for black opera singers is not much better. George Shirley, one of the only two Afro-American male singers ever to become regular members of the Metropolitan Opera—Robert McFerrin was the other—revealed that the Met's 1970–71 roster, now the leader in representation of blacks, stands at five to 136, while there are only five blacks in the opera chorus. Although Shirley does not say so, there are no blacks in the Metropolitan Opera orchestra.

While there are well-established graduate programs in ethnomusicology in some graduate schools, graduate instruction in black music in the public institutions of New York City is still practically nonexistent. The Graduate Center of the City University of New York which offers a Ph.D. program in historical musicology has no black students enrolled at the time of this writing and offers no courses in any area of Afro-American music, African music, Latin and Caribbean music, or ethnomusicology. This is true despite the fact that many of its graduates will undoubtedly seek teaching positions in community colleges where the largest numbers of black students in the City University of New York are concentrated.

Some liberal arts colleges have recently granted more flexibility to freshmen and sophomores by permitting them wider latitude in their choice of basic education courses—music, literature, art, philosophy, and foreign language—thereby giving them the option of electing other courses in the humanities in lieu of a formerly required course in music appreciation. Many other colleges, however, have not been disposed to such liberality and, throughout the country, literally thousands of college students are still required to enroll in music appreciation courses to meet degree requirements.

For many black college students from the nation's ghettos, these courses, rigidly steeped in the cultural tradition of Western Europe, are often fraught with prodigious difficulties. A close study of some of the latest textbooks written specifically for required music appreciation courses—and there is apparently a bull market for them—will enable us to understand and appreciate some of the difficulties black students might face in these types of music courses.

For this study, I have examined a dozen of the most current and widely used music appreciation texts in colleges and universities throughout the country.

To begin with, all these texts are designed to foster the appreciation of Western art music, and like the New York City syllabus, they virtually ignore black music and music of other cultures. Interestingly enough, Richard L. Crocker and Ann P. Basart in their *Listening to Music* frankly and openly attribute their omission of black music and non-Western music to their ignorance of the subject:

> WHY NO ROCK OR FOLK MUSIC? The authors have nothing against rock or folk—or jazz either. We just don't know enough about these repertories to write informatively about them . . . WHY NO ETHNIC MUSIC? Again our answer is that we have selected examples of the kind of music we know best.

I am sure that ignorance of the subject is probably one of the *real* reasons why most authors of music appreciation texts have either ignored black music altogether or have treated it slightly. But unlike Crocker and Basart, they are not candid or honest enough to admit it.

On the other hand, Jack Sacher (Montclair State College) and James Eversole (University of Connecticut), the coauthors of *The Art of Sound,* apparently unwilling to admit their ignorance of black music or their lack of concern for it, gave unconvincing rationalizations for their heavy emphasis on Western art music:

> The discussions have been confined to compositions produced within the so-called Western societies—Europe, Russia, and the Americas. This is intended neither as a slight to other societies and cultures nor as a suggestion that Western music is better than other music. The limitations of space in this book and of time in a one-semester course in music have forced this kind of focus. The student who wishes to explore the musical art of other societies is referred to section 10 of the Bibliography . . .

What Sacher and Eversole seem to be saying to black students here is, "If you want to explore your own musical heritage, find out about it yourself on your own time. We don't have time to bother with it because Western music is much more important." The author's excuses are thoroughly unconvincing, and black students will not fail to question their motives for omitting any discussion of the world's black music from their textbook.

Though most of the other music appreciation texts do not make such a pointed issue of their heavy concentration on Western European art music, the tables of contents of all of them nevertheless show beyond the slightest doubt that the emphasis does, in fact, lie in that area.

The difficulties that black students experience in traditionally oriented music appreciation courses are often compounded by the negative attitudes toward them of some of the professors who teach the courses. Some professors, for example, equate the understandable indifference of many black students to a music course which deals exclusively in Western art music with failure, while they ignore the very real possibility that if they place the right emphasis upon the black musical heritage, it would more than likely make a considerable difference in the interest and motivation of these students to deal successfully with the course as a whole. In this connection, Professor Machlis' (Queens College) attitudes on student evaluation, presented in the Instructor's Manual to his extremely popular text *The Enjoyment of Music,* are highly instructive:

> If, as a result of his being exposed to [western art] music in the basic course, he begins to buy records, attends concerts, listens to programs of serious music on the radio—if, in effect, he carries away from the course a love of music that will nourish him for the rest of his life, we have succeeded with him regardless of whether he has learned the "facts" or not. Contrariwise, if nothing has happened inside him to make him want to hear music, he obviously has failed the course . . .

This, of course, places the burden of responsibility for the course squarely on the shoulders of the student, ignoring the vital role that the professor must play in motivating his students and in making his course interesting, relevant, and meaningful. And furthermore, in the case of black students, who more than likely have had little prior exposure or interest in Western art music, how realistic is it to suppose that after a one-semester course in music appreciation, they will rush out and buy recordings of the Beethoven symphonies, or that they will now be "nourished" by Mozart for the rest of their lives?

As was the case with the New York City syllabus, most of these texts tended to create the impression (from their general tone and coverage) that the only significant musical contributions of blacks to American music are in the areas of spirituals and jazz, and that black composers have not been active in the composition of what they term "serious" music. Therefore, the works of blacks writing in the forms of Western art music are all but totally ignored just as they were in the New York City syllabus.

While generally agreeing that spirituals and jazz do in fact comprise the most significant contributions of blacks, Professor Machlis does at least mention, albeit ever so briefly, the names of four of the older and better known black composers—William Grant Still, Ulysses Kay, Howard Swanson, Julia Perry—in a single paragraph. Even though this is the only text examined that bothered to mention black composers at all, it is difficult to understand why Professor Machlis failed at least to mention any of the younger black composers whose works not only compare favorably with the four older black composers that he called attention to, but with the works of many of their more highly touted white contemporaries as well.

By excluding the works of black composers, the authors of these texts are either implying that black composers are so insignificant that they do not deserve even the briefest mention, or that they do not exist. These are most dangerous falsehoods, for they perpetuate the long standing myth so prevalent among white Americans that blacks lack the "aptitude" and "cultivation" to be outstanding performers of Western art music.

Not too long ago, Irving Kolodin, one of America's most respected music critics, overtly expressed this view in a critical review of the noted black pianist Andre Watts:

> So far as recollection serves, Watts is the first instrumentalist of Negro descent to earn such an honor with the Philharmonic. [Black] Vocalists, of course, there have been in abundance . . . But the blend of aptitude and cultivation that makes for the outstanding instrumentalist has hitherto eluded them. This may relate to the particular blend that has produced Watts, for his mother was Hungarian by birth.

As an interesting sidelight, let us look at a very similar statement written by Thomas Jefferson in 1803, when overt racism was just as fashionable an ideology as democracy:

> In music they [blacks] are more generally gifted than the
> whites with accurate ears for tune and time, and they have
> been found capable of imagining a small catch. Whether
> they will be equal to the composition of a more extensive
> run of melody, or of complicated harmony, is yet to be
> proved.

In comparing these two statements, it becomes immediately
apparent that over the past century and a half, racist myths
regarding the musical abilities of blacks have become thoroughly institutionalized and there are many contemporary
music educators, scholars, and critics who are not exempt
from its vicious effects. Examples of this may be seen in the
racist concepts which not infrequently appear in music appreciation textbooks, and which have in no small measure
contributed to the demands of black students for courses in
black music as viable substitutes for traditionally oriented
music appreciation courses.

Two egregious instances immediately come to mind. The
first, appearing in *A History of Art and Music* by H. W.
Janson (New York University) and Joseph Kerman (University of California, Berkeley), is one of the most disparaging
statements on jazz that I have seen in contemporary educational literature:

> Traditional music [Western art music] is middle class in
> orientation and is regarded as "cultural" and edifying
> while jazz is low class, strictly for fun, and often linked
> with dancing, courtship, and sex. Traditional music is
> deliberate, a composer's art preserved in a written score;
> jazz is spontaneous, a performer's art preserved only on
> records. The danger that traditional music runs is getting
> rarefied in the ivory tower. The danger that jazz runs is
> getting dirty in the market place . . . In harmony, pulse,
> musical form, and range of expression, most persons with
> extensive musical experience find jazz comparatively mea-
> ger, once the initial "kicks" have worn off . . . Jazz is a

minor art having its own integrity and liveliness, and probably it cannot bend too far without losing many of its characteristic virtues.

In the second example, Charles R. Hoffer (Indiana University) in *The Understanding of Music* revives the tired old "white-to-black" theory of the origins of Afro-American spirituals, which, as we have seen, is perennially resurrected by white scholars who simply cannot bring themselves to believe that "savage" and "primitive" black slaves could possibly have created this great body of noble song. Hoffer's treatment of the spirituals dovetails neatly with that of the New York City syllabus and to anyone who is familiar with both white and Afro-American spirituals, his observation that white spirituals are more "lyrical" and "polished" than Afro-American spirituals cannot possibly be based on anything more than his personal preference. The corroboration of Hoffer and the authors of the New York City syllabus on the "white-to-black" origins of the spirituals is not coincidental. The same theory appears with alarming regularity in textbook after textbook and in the works of some of the most highly respected musicologists. Homer Ulrich (University of Maryland), a distinguished musical scholar, gives credence to it in his text *Music: A Design for Listening*. The continued propagation of this racist theory is symptomatic of the almost compulsive need of many white scholars to minimize and belittle the musical contributions of blacks and to discredit the work of other scholars, both black and white, whose researches confirm that African retentions in the spirituals outweigh any other subsequent influences. I have already cited the works of these scholars.

A relatively new feature in the more recent music appreciation texts is the inclusion of brief chapters on either folk music, ethnic music, or jazz. Under normal circumstances, this might be viewed as a progressive and encouraging step forward, but close scrutiny of the contents of these chapters confirms the view that they are nothing more than token responses to the strong criticism of black faculty and students that up to now music appreciation texts have ignored the black musical experience in America.

The chapters on ethnic music in Hoffer's *The Understanding of Music,* Gillespie's *The Musical Experience,* and Nadeau and Tesson's *Listen: A Guide to the Pleasures of Music* are obviously included to appease black students and are so superficial and cursory in treatment that they call for no further critical discussion here.

The chapters on jazz, while not faring much better in quality, are at least more extensive in their coverage of the material. Most of them are brief historical summaries attempting to force the entire history of jazz into neat little captioned cubicles of three or four paragraphs each. In some of them, the level of writing is particularly banal and vapid, such as the beginning of the short paragraph that Hoffer devotes to his miniscule discussion of bebop, one of the most crucial styles in the entire history of jazz:

> Following World War II there emerged a style called *bebop,* or more commonly, *bop.* It was developed chiefly by Charlie "Bird" Parker and Dizzy Gillespie, who once defined the term by saying that in bop you go *Ba*-oo *Ba*-oo *Ba*-oo instead of *Oo*-ba *Oo*-ba *Oo*-ba.

But the real problems that have made the jazz world a living hell on earth for black jazzmen are studiously avoided —problems such as "unemployment, lack of due recognition, . . . lack of proper distribution and advertising publicity for recordings, inability to be recorded, the inference that jazz is not serious music, because the greatest innovators have been black, and since the music comes out of ghettos, it can be worth only so much as a viable, indigenous art form."

Just as it is impossible to understand fully the music of Beethoven or Mozart without a thorough consideration of the momentous social forces which shaped their lives and times, it is impossible to understand jazz without considering such factors as the pervasive and corrosive racism that transformed Louis Armstrong from one of the most original innovators in the entire history of jazz into a veritable stereotype of himself, or the mobster-ridden, narcotics-infested, alcohol-drenched "garbage can" milieu of the jazz club in which the genius of Charlie Parker and John Coltrane blazed with such incandescent brilliance, and which ultimately led to Parker's tragic and untimely death at the height of his musical powers. These tragic stories could be repeated a thousandfold out of context, but without probing their significance to the music and to the men who made that music, the true meaning of jazz can never be communicated, no matter how deft the musical analysis or how scholarly the bare historical facts of jazz styles are set down by white critics who refuse to face the nasty, exploitative realities inherent in the history of black jazz.

In summation, then, music appreciation textbooks, like the New York City syllabus, minimize the black musical experience in America by drastically limiting the extent and quality of its coverage and by questioning its suitability as an independent field of scholarly inquiry. As is the case in practically all other areas of American life, black music is segregated from the mainstream of American music in these texts—conveniently tucked away into separate but unequal chapters. But what is most striking here is the shabby treatment of black music by white authors whose commitment to and knowledge of it leaves much to be desired. In the face of this, one wonders why black musical scholars, black composers, or black musicians, whose knowledge and experience uniquely qualify them to speak with authority on the subject, have not been consulted, or why the bibliographies of music appreciation texts contain virtually no references to the works of black scholars.

The highly unsatisfactory treatment of black music in these texts is undoubtedly due to the ignorance of the subject by white scholars resulting from the long history of condemnation and denigration of black music by the elitist American educational Establishment. As a natural consequence of this, music education in America for both blacks and whites has not reflected the black musical experience as blacks perceive or experience it. Years of colonization, enslavement, and exploitation of blacks by Europeans and Americans have so firmly implanted the stigma of black inferiority in the minds of whites that they find it difficult to concede the existence of any real black cultural values except in the most condescending and disparaging sense. As a result, whites have distorted and subverted the black musical experience, transforming it into a hideous parody of itself through such sick manifestations as their blackface minstrels, their Al Jolsons, their Elvis Presleys, and their beloved *Porgy and Bess* and *Carmen Jones.*

No one knows this better than today's black youth and it is they who will ultimately force the issue. During the 1969–70 school year, it suddenly became clear to black students throughout the land, especially those in predominantly white colleges and universities, that "this version of the black man's existence in America was at best a misconception and was probably a deliberate falsehood invented by racist elements in our society, who employed willing universities and colleges to perpetuate its myth."

Realization led to confrontations in which black students demanded courses which dealt with the black experience in a truthful, relevant manner. In the field of music, this led to demands for separate courses in black music which would deal with the black musical experience from a black point of view. At last black students had come to know that traditional music courses had failed to provide learning experiences relevant to blacks and that the root cause of that failure was racism.

The music appreciation texts that I have examined continue that failure. In fact, they justify the demands of black students for separate courses in black music. However, in a pluralistic society such as ours, it is more preferable to have a music curriculum that reflects the musical cultures of all elements of that society. But until white music educators realize this and are willing to modify their textbooks, their curricula, and, above all, their negative attitudes toward the music of other cultures, music courses dealing exclusively with the black experience, taught from a black point of view, should and must be made available as an expedient against the time when music will be taught as the universal language of the *entire* world rather than as the provincial language of the white peoples of the Western world.

5

The Militant Separatists in the White Academy

by William J. Harris

Mr. Harris was born on a farm a few miles outside of Yellow Springs, Ohio, on March 12, 1942. When he was three, his parents moved to Yellow Springs where they opened a small appliance store. His education through high school included informal teaching by beatniks. For the past four years he has been a graduate student at Stanford University, where he studied British and American literature. He has published in several magazines, among them The Antioch Review, The Beloit Poetry Journal, The American Scholar, *and in a number of anthologies, such as* Nine Black Poets, New Black Voices, Natural Process *and others. At present he is a doctoral candidate in English at Stanford University and is writing a book on LeRoi Jones's poetry. He is now teaching creative writing and American literature at Cornell University.*

The influences of black separatism have seeped into surprising places in the American empire: the white academy and the "integrated" world of letters. The blacks in these communities are a select class who have been favored by white society—the students, intellectuals and creative writers who have been given all the prizes. Yet, even among these favored people, there are strong separatist feelings.

The university, my world, is a place of symbolic criticism

of our society, a stage where the young, with a few older friends, act out society's dramas in the open. It is a microcosm for the more veiled and secretive world beyond the ivory towers. I think that, by watching this drama carefully, one can understand much about our country. Whether this is the case or not, this is my stage, my world, my place to watch.

Separatism has entered my daily life in the white university. Its main effect has been not to create in most blacks an overwhelming desire to go back to Africa or to build a great black nation below the Mason-Dixon line or even to cease talking to white people, but to shift the emphasis of the black movement from freedom to identity. The university has traditonally been a place of questioning, and it has become a place where identity is a major issue for every student, white or black. Separatism makes the question of identity a little easier for black students. Blacks alone with other blacks can talk things out, can work out common problems "in the family."

The greatest impact of separatism has been on the younger members of the family—blacks under forty. Most older blacks are militantly against it. Most younger blacks are militantly for it. They are more divided over separatism than militancy. Even Martin Luther King could understand (if not accept) the destruction of the cities, but not separatism. The old not only have seen progress but they have gained a sense of history merely by living; they have something against which to judge the militant rhetoric. The young have only their handful of years and their innocence. They have not yet been molded by experience; therefore, the immediate moment makes a great impression on them because that is all they know. Because they are inexperienced, they are romantic and believe themselves unlimited. So when the latest revolutionary brother tells them that they are African princes, they become African princes.

This propensity for total identification is not restricted to young blacks. In fact, Gary Snyder, the white guru of young WASP America, can convince an auditorium full of white students that he is an Indian and that they are not white—that they, too, are Indians—and are free from the white guilt. At one point recently in a conversation with a group of white students at Stanford, Snyder said, "We aren't Indian (from India). We must look to our own land for answers. Look at the American Indian." I know that what Snyder meant was that the native American has wisdom that we can learn from, but it is so easy for young people with poorly defined self-images to confuse studying the Indian with being the Indian. At least the black student is black, and by playing an African prince he may be working toward some kind of true identity, but the white kid playing that he is an Indian is only fooling himself. A few years ago he was a hippie, before that a Zen Buddhist. Then he protested for a while to escape white America, but the Great White Machine proved hard to destroy. In the university he was a new-style radical whose main psychopolitical function was to destroy his father's house, crying, "I am not white, I am not white. I destroy the white man's property."

Now the very youngest generation has invented a new escape from the white guilt: go back in time and pretend the blacks don't exist. Go back to the forties and fifties before there were niggers in every other TV commercial, go back to the ducktail and Howdy Doody, go back before the Vietnam war. Pretend that you are the son in "Father Knows Best." Wear white bucks, fall in love with the WASP next door, play mad practical jokes (never talk politics). Nostalgia can protect you. Go back, go back before the blacks ever existed. And study, study, study. Study, as you never studied before, to escape the blacks, the war, life. On a recent visit to several colleges, I heard over and over, "the kids are back to the books." They will do anything to escape the white guilt, except face themselves.

But they must face their whiteness, accept it even though it is not exotic. They, as well as the blacks, want to escape the burning house of America. They see that the country is lost; they hear what the avant-garde has been saying at least since the 1950s: the West is spiritually bankrupt.

But the black man cannot go back to the 1950s because he did not exist in the 1950s. The black intellectual was totally integrated into the burning house. There was the great Western tradition and it was good and that was what you learned in school. No matter what your background, you were expected to become a white Anglo-Saxon.

The Jewish writer Norman Podhoretz expresses the common plight of the minority intellectual in those years. He faces the question of ethnic identity; he has two schools to go to, one Jewish, one WASP:

> When I was in college the term WASP had not yet come into currency—which is to say that the realization had not yet become widespread that white Americans of Anglo-Saxon Protestant background are an ethnic group like any other, that their characteristic qualities are by no means self-evidently superior to those of the other groups, and that neither their earlier arrival nor their majority status entitles them to exclusive possession of the national identity. In the absence of this realization, Columbia had no need to be as fully conscious of the social implications of the purposes it was pursuing as, on its side, the Seminary necessarily was. The demand being made on me as a student of Jewish culture was concrete, explicit, and unambiguous: "Become a good Jew!" The demand being made on me as a student of Western Culture, by contrast, was seductively abstract and idealized: "Become a gentleman, a man of enlightened and gracious mind!" It is not that Columbia was being dishonest in failing to mention

that this also meant "Become a facsimile WASP!" In taking that corollary for granted, the college was simply being true to its own ethnic and class origins; and in nothing did this fidelity show itself more clearly than in the bland unconsciousness that accompanied it.

If you wanted to be an intellectual you had to forget your ethnic past and enter the wonderful world of white letters. Ideas were white. The black man thought about personal freedom but didn't think about identity. He wrote and talked like a white man: James Baldwin wrote like Henry James. I remember in the late 1950s arguing with a Polish friend about ethnic identity. He argued that without ethnic traditions people would be dreary and all alike. I countered that if there were going to be any peace in the world we had to give up ethnic distinctions and be brothers. As George Romney said after his trip to Vietnam: I was brainwashed.

It was not very important to me that I was a black. Blacks at that time weren't proud of their past. I was very proud of my family—but I was an American and being black was of little consequence. What impressed me about Baldwin was that he saw that he was an American when he got to Europe. The simple fact that one could be both an American and a black never dawned on me. We were just Americans with dark skins. As LeRoi Jones says, "Africa is a foreign place."

The shift in feeling from the 1950s to the present is extraordinary. In the fifties we wanted to be imitation white men (of course, this was an unconscious desire): "The West was best." The majority was right without question, but those years are over. Now we feel that if we ever come back to an integrated house it must be as blacks with a distinct but equal culture. Mozart must make room for John Coltrane. A vital people cannot be imitations of anybody else. They must be themselves.

There is some truth in the idea of killing the father for independence. Baldwin had to kill Wright, and Cleaver had to kill Baldwin. Now the young blacks are killing the white race to escape it. When LeRoi Jones says that Dante (one of his old culture heroes) is nothing but a copy of some obscure Arab, he is killing the white man in himself—which is healthier than killing the black man in himself.

For the moment it may be psychologically necessary for people in the black community to see black people as the only hope for black people—to see black people as the new saints and white people as devils. The white man must be totally evil so blacks can be freed from him. They must harden their hearts against him and dehumanize him so that he can be exorcised. This is a psychic war in which the black man is fighting for his life. The white man has denied him his culture. It doesn't matter whether the act was conscious or not. He has said that all civilization is white by his actions, attitudes and words. If you write a book about civilizations and don't mention black people you are denying that they have ever done anything. You are denying their importance by silence. The black man is destroyed by this silence. It is an easy thing to do. I have done it and it has been done to me.

The town I was reared in was a liberal place. It actually believed in the equality and brotherhood of man—at least a good number of the townspeople did. A small town in southwestern Ohio, which was once a station on the underground railroad, it is still an oasis of liberalism in a desert of conservatism. But what is important for our purposes about this town is that the good liberal people were involved in the racism of silence. They believed in brotherhood, but it was unconsciously white brotherhood. The townspeople were saying silently: "We will love you no matter what the color of your skin is if you act like us."

It is endlessly more complicated than this but, in essence, this good town denied me my racial past. I grew up with no sense of blackness. The only definitions around me were white. I went to a white school, talked to white people, went with white girls, read white books, and was white. I was a white liberal. Sister Nikki Giovanni is wrong when she says, "A Black man living at the North Pole is still a Black man— with African roots, with a Black, hence African, way of look- ing at his life, of ordering his world, or relating to his dreams, of responding to his environment." A black man is only a black man when he has black models to emulate and I didn't have any. The whites did not intentionally try to make me white, but that is what happened.

The traditions I grew up with were white. LeRoi Jones says: "Having read all of whitie's books, I wanted to be an authority on them. Having been taught that art was 'what white men did,' I almost became one, to have a go at it." There were blacks in my school, but they were not interested in what I was interested in. The whites had taught me that the mind—culture—was good, and the black kids weren't in- terested in things of the mind. I was a poet, and they were basketball players. I felt comfortable talking to people who were interested in the things I was, and these people in- variably were white. In high school I read Joyce, Beckett, Pound, Kerouac and Baldwin (not Wright, of course, he was too black, too provincial). I read white and almost-white writers because they spoke about my life. The only black writer I read (Baldwin) talked in a language I understood. I was white, as a black at the North Pole would be a North Polean (?) or a penguin.

When I taught a class of chicanos and blacks, I was guilty of the racism of silence. Since I was a midwesterner, I knew nothing about chicanos, I devoted the class to black and white literature. We only talked about black problems in the class, for I assumed that chicanos had the same problems as blacks. The chicano students accepted it because they had not reached the level of consciousness to reject it. The fol- lowing year the next group of chicano freshmen demanded that they have a chicano teacher. I was a man of goodwill, but I was forcing the chicano to define himself in my black terms.

The young blacks are facing themselves or at least trying to face themselves. Racial identity has become a real question for them. A characteristic of new movements is that the first answers tend to be stupid and narrow. But they create a climate for new answers. And I hope a genius will come along with some good answers we can all use. A round-faced black youth said to his black teacher the other day, "I want to develop a black philosophy." Ten years ago he would have wanted to develop a new Western philosophy. But I must not be to cynical, because maybe he will. The great thing about the young is that they do not know it is almost impossible to do grand things.

There are a variety of opinions about separatism in the black community. Jim Simmons, assistant to the president of Stanford University, thinks "it's an important stage for black people to get themselves together." On the other hand, Sara Parkinson, a black student at Stanford, thinks it's more than a stage: it is a matter of black survival. She believes that America is going to try to put the blacks in concentration camps and murder them and that to stay in this country would be suicide. Implicit in Jim Simmons' position is that America is well-meaning even if misguided. I would imagine that he could not take too seriously the King Alfred Plan from John A. Williams' novel, *The Man Who Cried I Am,* "to detain and ultimately rid America of its Negroes." I know that I could not when I first read the book. I found it a major flaw that took us away from the real problems of blacks, placing us in a paranoid fantasy world of black genocide. Yet one's sense of reality is flimsy: the real is more a matter of repetition than actuality. Just because you cannot visualize something doesn't mean it isn't true but may mean only that your range of experience is too limited. When the young militant tells us that gas chamber *satori* is in our future, we shouldn't dismiss it totally. Samuel F. Yette's *The Choice* tells us that the Community Action Program, an agency of the United States government, has been "a name-taking web that helped identify and isolate natural leaders of every black community in America, each leader's name ultimately fixed to a massive pickup list at the Pentagon" and that a committee of the House of Representatives has made recommendations on methods of isolating and destroying black citizens if they get out of hand. These items are not fictions from a novel but are facts from Yette's well-documented nonfiction book about black genocide. If we have any concern about our survival, we must take these facts seriously, which is very difficult when you spend most of your days talking to genteel and humane men about British and American literature.

A frightening question is, if the United States decides to liquidate the black population, who is to stop them? A few snipers with .22s shouting Black Power? Sara Parkinson's mistrust of America is shared by many other young blacks. The possibility, the immediacy, of genocide is more real to them than it is to me. Often these are the people who would receive the American prizes (good jobs, big houses, et cetera) but they are no longer interested. It isn't going to do Charles Gordone any good that he won the Pulitzer Prize if he is in a gas chamber. Listen to the Jew Lowenthal in Stanley Kramer's film, *Ship of Fools;* the time is just before the Second World War:

> . . . We're German first, and Jew second. We've done so much for Germany, Germany has done so much for us, what are we supposed to do—pack up our bags and leave because of a few trouble-makers? . . . Listen. There are six million of us. What are they going to do? Kill all of us?

The happy *Sambo* nigger has been replaced by the militant nigger. We are not all eighteen years old and we should know better, but some of us have let ourselves be fooled and

cheapened by American civilization. We have accepted sim-
plified images of our black selves. We have believed in some
dark corner of our minds that we are Douglas V. Militant,
letting our entire essence be defined by that role. A couple
of years before we were Sidney P. Genius, neurosurgeon and
astrophysicist, and before there were any blacks in the national consciousness, we were the Lone Ranger—not native
American Tonto. Everybody tells us what black is. We have
been told that black is beautiful and I agree. But black is
also vastly complicated, and it seems that black people at
least should realize this even if whites do not. Black people
in this country come from many cultures and backgrounds;
there is no monolithic black culture. By going Home, back
to our black identities, we have a great chance to get back
to our roots and escape old stereotypes, but realities are too
frightening for most people, and they only want new stereotypes to replace the old ones. To the question of what is
blackness, we must have 22,000,000 answers.

When blackness is too narrowly and mechanically defined,
the black community—especially in the university—becomes
a stifling and neurotic place. Let us listen to black students
who have had difficulties because of inflexible definitions of
blackness.

A Princeton student said to me: "At school I found out
that the kids who had the greatest identity crises were the
black students from the middle or upper class. . . . They
were very insecure in their blackness and came on very strong
about being black. I had to learn that their hangups weren't
mine. I didn't romanticize the brother on the block, I knew
him—almost got beaten up by him."

A middle-class black student talks of her difficulties in becoming "black":

> It's hard if you haven't grown up in a Black community.
> You feel really inhibited . . . you don't have the same
> social skills that the other Black kids have naturally be-
> cause they have grown up with blackness and you have

to gain these skills . . . and sometimes you feel you have to try a little harder and sometimes you are rejected and you don't understand why because you are Black.

Sandy Packard, another student, talks about how she had to change herself to be accepted. "When I arrived at Stanford the Black students told me I wasn't Black enough for them . . . said I talked like a white person and thought I must have straightened my hair." This student is a Jamaican who has spent several years in England and who had a British accent. She continues:

> I tried to kink up my hair for awhile. I was rejected by the Black kids for the first year. But then I lost my accent. It's strange how that happened. While I was in a play— a Black play—the director told me over and over: "If you are going to play a Black woman you can't talk like a white woman." Well, I lost my accent and the Blacks now accept me.

Commenting on Sandy's situation, the Princeton student said: "These kids who gave her a hard time weren't being intentionally cruel or hard-boiled. They were suffering with their own wounds. Doubt is hard to keep to yourself."

Many young middle-class blacks feel unauthentic because they do not come from the ghetto. Being brought up in white or imitation-white worlds, they are bitter about being deprived of their black pasts. Instead of regarding themselves as privileged, as they once would have, they think of themselves as freaks cut off from their blackness. Exploring one aspect of this attitude is Nancy McCormick in her poem, "Black Misery":

> Black misery is having everybody in
> your white school know your name
> because you are so identifiable
> and not knowing the kid who
> just said, "Hi!"

Black pride has been an important aspect of the separatist position. The separatist says: "If you love yourself, you should want to stay with your own people: don't run off to those white neighborhoods and stop running around with those white gals." Black people should take themselves seriously—believe they are important enough to talk to and to love. It was depressing back at Ohio's Central State University when my black male friends would say: "If I want somebody to talk to me, I got to run over to the white college and find myself a white girl." But it is fanatical to say that you can only talk to black people, and it appears that some blacks are afraid that whites have more to say than blacks.

Yet it is important for black people to be proud. I have spent hours fighting with Paul, an African friend, about American black pride. A little drunk, his eyes nearly closed, calling the black waitress Mother, Paul said: "Nobody has to tell the lion that he is beautiful and should be proud of his lion-ness. He doesn't need Lion-tude." "Yeah," I replied, seeing that the waitress looked a little like my mother, "but nobody has told the lion for three hundred years that he is inferior." Langston Hughes is right when he says: "Wear it [color] / Like a banner / For the proud." And Don L. Lee is wrong when he says: "I / began to love / only a / part of / me—my inner / self which / is all / black—& developed a / vehement hatred of / my light / brown / outer." Paradoxically, Lee's light brown skin is part of his blackness—his individual blackness—which should not be rejected.

Blackness is both a political and cultural fact. We are black politically because, even though we are individuals, we are treated collectively; therefore, it is important for our well-being that we stick together. We shouldn't need a crisis as serious as genocide to move us to collective action. Blacks may simply go out of fashion. Even though it is an over-statement to say that we were ever in fashion, we have definitely gone out of style before. The Depression destroyed the white man's enthusiasm for the New Negro and the writers of the Harlem Renaissance, and no great interest in blacks and their literature developed again until civil rights and black power appeared on the scene.

There are signs that black literature is finished as a commercial commodity: according to the reports I hear, sales are down. So it is fortunate that we have set up our own presses (even if they are small) for they will continue publishing black writers out of a commitment. This is great for the writers, but presses are not the backbone of a community. We need other black institutions (cultural and economic). The only people who are going to care about black people (if there are any, and I'm not sure there are) over a long period of time are black people; hence, we need our own institutions to insure our survival.

The separatist attitude has had both good and bad effects on the black community. It has created a positive climate for thought. With hundreds of young blacks wanting to create a black philosophy, something must come of it. It has made black students want to go back to the ghetto instead of escaping it; many young blacks are becoming lawyers and doctors in order to be useful to their community. While at school many blacks go back (or for the first time go) into the community to help their black brothers and sisters. Separatism has made blacks want to define themselves in their own terms—not those of other people.

It is beneficial to be able to go home, but people tend to be very narrow if they know only their own hometown. There is a world outside the city limits waiting to be discovered. I hope that militant separatism is only a stage in which we as black people learn to love ourselves. Later, I hope we can enter into a truly integrated world—a multiracial world where people can be different from one another without terrifying one another, where people can "respect each other for their own thing," as B. B. King says. But as this vision of racial harmony passes before my eyes, I see my militant brother giving me a look of total disbelief at my naïveté.

A *Muhammad Speaks* hawker comes up. Smiles.

"Brother," he says, "what's your major?"

"English. American Lit."

"Oh, that doesn't go back too far—about a hundred and seventy years, Emerson and Thoreau."

"Yeah."

He shoves the *Speaks* in my face. "Look at the back page. See what we are building in Phoenix—a community business center." He reaches out his hand.

Almost unconsciously, I hand him my weekly quarter.

"Ah, brother," he asks, in his most beautifully sarcastic tones, "what are you building?"